A Pathfinder's Story

A Pathfinder's Story

The Life and Death of Jack Mossop
DFC* DFM

Bill Robinson

Pen & Sword
AVIATION

First published in Great Britain in 2007 by
Pen & Sword Aviation
an imprint of
Pen & Sword Books Ltd
47 Church Street
Barnsley
South Yorkshire
S70 2AS

A CIP catalogue record for this book is
available from the British Library

Typeset in 11/13pt Sabon by
Lamorna Publishing Services

Printed and bound in England by CPI UK.

For a complete list of Pen & Sword titles please contact
PEN & SWORD BOOKS LIMITED
47 Church Street, Barnsley, South Yorkshire, S70 2AS, England
E-mail: enquiries@pen-and-sword.co.uk
Website: www.pen-and-sword.co.uk

Contents

Acknowledgements

Although I have made good use of other works written about the RAF bomber campaign, as indicated in the notes, the story of Jack and Hilda Mossop could not have been told without five essential sources.

First – the National Archives at Kew, whose staff were exemplary in providing assistance and advice on how to identify and locate the principal sources and provided access to the Operational Books of the RAF stations on which Jack Mossop served during his three operational tours. The files consulted were AIR 27 and AIR 28.

Second – the Ministry of Civil Aviation file on the accident to Lancastrian G-AGMF, reference BT217, now held by the National Archives.

Third – the Royal Air Force Personnel Agency at RAF Innsworth who provided details of Jack Mossop's career.

Fourth – the library of the RAF Museum at Hendon where, with expert advice from the staff, I was able to understand the internal layout of various aircraft in which Jack Mossop flew.

And Fifth – information provided by Bill Lloyd and his daughter Jenny Coster on the complements of the crews on 76 and 35 Squadrons and their exploits. Beryl Hill, the widow of Warrant Officer Cliff Hill, also provided memories of Jack Mossop, and my cousin, Mary Fawcett, gave me information on the relationships in the Mossop family.

I must also acknowledge the help I have had from my family, in particular of course from my mother, Hilda, whose memory over more than sixty years is better than mine over one, and also from my son, Daniel, who contributed much to the structure of the story and provided some invaluable proof reading.

This story is dedicated to all aircrew of the RAF, RCAF and BOAC who flew with Jack Mossop.

Introduction

I am going to tell you a tragic story; a story of love, too much war, too little peace and a sad death. The story is based on facts so far as I know them, but whereas the facts about war are, in general, well recorded, the facts about peace and love are often hidden. You will find, therefore, that most of this book tells the story of one man's experience of war and its aftermath. The story of the love between that man and a woman is more quickly told, but told it must be, for without that love I would not be here to tell it. Love is an antidote to the poison of war, but only the fortunate find it, and even in peace there is uncertainty and risk.

Behind the main tragic theme you will find a number of lesser themes: love, bravery, politics, strategy, technology, Canadians, bombing operations and, rising above all the others, risk. Risk of death, risk of injury, risk of capture, risk of illness, risk brought about through the need for battle in war. In peace the risk is of a lesser degree than in war, but we will see that the consequences of a hazardous event can still be fatal.

The war which forms the backcloth to the greater part of this story is the Second World War, which lasted in Europe from 3 September 1939 to 7 May 1945. The people of Great Britain and of the British Empire and Commonwealth toiled throughout the war in all its theatres, providing for part of the time the only opposition to the expansionist axis of Germany and Italy. In 1940, with France beaten, it seemed inevitable that northern Europe would fall under German rule. The opportunist attack by Japan on Pearl Harbor late in 1941 brought the might of the USA into the war and it became possible that the Western Allies might, at least, not lose the war. However, the battles which would win the war were not fought until 1944. By chance 1944 was also the year in which love, between the two main protagonists in this story, led to marriage. As for death, it is never far away in the story, and in the end it proves its power. I will not begin at the beginning because I would like first to explain how things stood in the crucial year of 1944.

Chapter 1

The Diary

The Collins Aero diary for the year 1944 had a notice on its first page:

> POSTAL INFORMATION
> For postal information, apply at local Post Office. When going to print it was decided to omit this section as it was impossible to say what postal rate would be in force in 1944.

Uncertainty was a condition of life in most of Europe at the beginning of 1944. After four years of war the once unstoppable military successes of German and Japanese forces had been checked, but at much cost, and it was by no means certain that crucial battles ahead would be won. The uncertainty applied at all levels. The alliance between the Western powers and the Soviet Union was driven by necessity rather than by common aspirations, as would be seen during the final battle for Berlin in 1945. Differing strategic aims would also lead to uncertainty at the planning level, whilst at the fighting level the dreadful risk of sudden death hung over all, including the civilian population of the United Kingdom.

Without doubt it was a year of uncertainty for Flying Officer Jack Mossop. He had survived two tours of operational duty flying in Hampden and Halifax aircraft, but now he was destined for a Lancaster squadron. More than that, he was destined for the Pathfinder Force, No. 8 Group of RAF Bomber Command. The Pathfinders' task was to mark the target of a raid with flares and then to ensure that the main force of bombers understood which markers should be used as the target for bombing. This

1

role was necessarily more hazardous because it required a Pathfinder to remain in the danger area over the target for longer time than the main force aircraft. So when Jack purchased his copy of the 1944 Collins Aero diary, uncertainty over the cost of a postage stamp would not have been his major concern. With two operational tours behind him Jack had already outlived more than half of the aircrew he had trained with. He had flown over enemy territory on fifty-four occasions and had earned a Distinguished Flying Medal (DFM) and a Distinguished Flying Cross (DFC). The DFM meant the more to him because the DFC was only awarded to commissioned officers and it was often said that they earned their decorations more easily than those in the other ranks. Also, he had earned his DFM early in the bombing campaign, when medals were less often awarded. He had been on a daylight operation to bomb a German military airfield. His two-engined Hampden was badly shot up by defensive fire, and it only just reached the English coast before it crash landed at Bircham Wood, the first airfield they could reach, after a perilous return flight with a mortally wounded navigator.

Whatever thoughts Jack Mossop might have about his chance of surviving another operational tour, a pocket diary specialising in aeronautical science would seem to be an excellent choice for an aviator. Indeed, there is an amazing level of detail in the 144 pages which precede the calendar section of the Collins Aero diary for 1944. For example, the topic of adiabatic compression and efficiency can be found on page 72, whilst the cooling of aircraft engines takes up four pages of tightly compressed text, graphs and drawings. These were of little interest to Jack because he had trained as a wireless operator. He had also qualified as an air gunner, and he was thus a member of the RAF aircrew community known as WOP/AGs. Later, he would also become a bomb-aimer. The 1944 Collins Aero diary avoids these aspects of military aeronautics; public knowledge of the application of what we would now call electronics, including radio, radar, and information processing, was almost non-existent given wartime restrictions on such information. Jack would have had little use for the technical section of the diary.

He seems neither to have been keen to use the diary in the conventional way of remembering appointments, keeping notes, and recording events. On the page provided for telephone numbers, only five lines are taken up. The first, Newcastle 25031, was the work number of Hilda Charlton, his fiancée, who had a job with a wood importing company. Next he wrote the number of the Three Tuns Hotel in Durham, where they had met. Then there is the number of the colliery in Medomsley where his future father-in-law worked as an engineer, followed by a Mrs Alexander, a neighbour of Hilda's parents who had a telephone. Finally, he entered the number of Uncle Sydney Walton in Whitley Bay. Two addresses appear on a page headed memoranda, one of a Mrs Hadscombe in Oxford, and the other of another member of the Walton family, Aunt Dolly, at 34 Evesham Avenue, Monkseaton, an area thought by some to be at the better end of Whitley Bay. Jack's only child would be born there in January 1945.

The first two pages of the calendar section, covering 1 to 13 January, have been torn out, so dated diary entries should begin on 14 January but they don't because, with few exceptions, Jack uses the diary only to record operations against the enemy. This story is in part based on those diary entries. Supported by the more sparse entries in his RAF Flying Log Book, the diary records one aviator's activities and thoughts during the critical phase of the Allies' bombing campaign against Germany, up to his last mission on Monday 8 August 1944. Preceding the events recorded in the diary there are, of course, the essential precursors; training, experience, and what most called luck. We shall see from events following 1944 that luck is merely a figment, an emotional illusion not related to the real and dispassionate matter of risk.

The scarcity of other entries in the diary may be explained by security considerations. The detailed recording of operations was almost certainly a breach of regulations, and Jack may have kept the diary hidden in his locker in the Officers' Mess. The neat writing and attention to detail would suggest that, with a few exceptions, the diary entries were written within a day or so of the activities they describe, rather than being scribbled in an aircraft returning from battle. Perhaps he had two diaries, one for general use, including the usual personal appointments, notes, addresses, and telephone numbers. This could explain the absence of the first two pages of the surviving diary – torn out when he decided that the trivia of daily life should kept in a separate diary, accessible when needed, the Collins Aero diary being secured in his locker for retrospective recording of his observations.

Having introduced Jack and Hilda, I may as well introduce myself as their son. As I won't appear in person for some time, I will try not to draw attention to myself. But now we should go back to the beginning and see how things stood in 1940.

Chapter 2

The War in 1940

At the onset of the Second World War in 1939 the concept of a military organisation dedicated to bombing an enemy was itself quite new. Bomber Command had been formed only three years previously, in 1936. Many, particularly in the Royal Navy and the British Army, thought it a waste of scarce resources. However, farsighted air marshals had won some battles in Whitehall, and modern aircraft had been ordered from the manufacturers in what became known as the RAF Expansion scheme. But no war had yet been fought in which air power on its own could achieve a long term strategic advantage. Nor had there been time to determine what tactics should be used to apply this strategic power. The prevailing view of the Royal Air Force (RAF) on the subject of bombing tactics was that a tight formation of bombers would be able to fight their way to an enemy target, and get back. This was the time when biplanes were still being replaced by more modern aircraft which were both faster and more able to defend themselves. Theorists suggested that when flying in formation, the new bombers, with their flexible gun turrets, would be able to fight off attacks from all quarters. Even if this theory was valid, it was only viable in daylight because in the dark it would have been impossible to maintain formation. In practice, it soon became apparent that fighters could easily penetrate the defensive shield, albeit with some losses and, in any case, the greater threat to the bomber was ground based anti-aircraft gunnery. Tight formation flying merely presented an easier target for the gunners. Marshal of the Royal Air Force Sir John Slessor, who was in charge of planning at the Air Ministry in 1937, said later:[1] 'Before 1939 we really knew nothing about air warfare.'

It was not that people had not tried. As Chief of the Air Staff in London, Lord Trenchard had kept the RAF viable during the retrenchment of the 1920s, but such was the lack of funds that the RAF's principal bomber in 1932 was the Vickers Virginia[2] – a two engine wooden biplane with an open cockpit and a top speed of 108 mph. Trust had mistakenly been placed in the Disarmament Conference, which met in Geneva from 1932 until it broke up in disarray in 1934.

When Adolf Hitler became Chancellor of Germany in January 1933 the die was set, even if few recognised it. Fortunately, the British Air Ministry had noticed the developments in aeronautics which the growing airline industry had generated. They had also noticed advances in the conduct of air warfare, particularly the use of aircraft to bomb both military and civilian targets during the Spanish Civil War, most notably when the German Condor Legion destroyed Guernica on 16 April 1937. There was some despondency over the general view, expressed by the Prime Minister, Stanley Baldwin, during a debate in the House of Commons on 10 November 1937, 'that the bomber will always get through' since the dictum obviously applied to the German Air Force, the *Luftwaffe*, as much as to the RAF. However, with financial controls loosened, some improvement became possible. First, contracts were let for Hurricane and Spitfire aircraft to defend British airspace. Then, radar systems were installed to detect enemy intruders and new bombers were also ordered. An Air Ministry Specification which had been issued as far back as December 1932 led, seven years later, to deliveries of the two-engined Vickers Wellington, popularly known as the Wimpey. The type entered service as the war began in 1939, and by the end of 1941 Bomber Command had twenty-one squadrons equipped and operational with the Wellington.

Another two-engined bomber, built to the same specification as the Wellington, the Handley Page Hampden, also came into service in 1939, and it would be the first type to carry Jack Mossop to war. But the limitations of two-engined bombers had, by then, been recognised. In an air battle, four engines are much better than two, both for manoeuvrability and for survivability

6

should an engine fail, and the greater power of four engines allows a heavier bomb load.

The first four-engined bomber to enter service was the Short Stirling in August, 1940. The Avro Lancaster, undoubtedly the best bomber of the Second World War, did not arrive until early in 1942.

So it was that the RAF found itself still re-arming when the war began on 3 September 1939. Nevertheless, air operations began immediately despite the restriction on Bomber Command, soon lifted, that it was allowed to drop bombs only on German warships. The futility of daylight raids on land targets was thus not at first recognised. Senior commanders continued to believe that a well-disciplined formation of bombers could beat off attacks by fighter aircraft. That belief was finally shattered on 18 December 1939, when a force of twenty-four Wellington bombers was caught by enemy fighters off the coast of Germany. Ten were shot down, and further eleven were damaged.[3] The decision to switch to night operations was perilous since crews had not been trained to fly in the dark, but it was a decision which had to be made. Sadly, beyond the mantra that the bomber would always get through, there was then no recognised and proven set of tactics for the deployment of a bomber force. Evidence in Abyssinia and Iraq, where the RAF had developed a policing role, indicated that bombers were most useful in a strategic role. The mere threat of bombing a recalcitrant village was sufficient to impress on lightly-armed forces the folly of resistance. The strategic value of simply having a squadron of bombers was then greater than any tactical value they may have had in battle. But now the cards were on the table. A bomber force had to be credible in the task of bombing the enemy's infrastructure as well as tactical targets on a battlefield or at sea. It must be able to attack strategic targets throughout the enemy's homeland, targets which were defended by heavily-armed forces. Late in 1939 and early in 1940 the RAF had hardly begun to create that credibility.

It was not just the need for more aircraft and aircrew. The new Wellingtons, Stirlings, and Hampdens were rolling off the production lines, and there was initially a good supply of pilots. But the new aircraft required new types of aircrew. Air Gunners were an immediate need, met initially by continuation of the RAF's simple expedient of putting armament fitters behind the guns which they had maintained and armed; they were given sixpence per day, the equivalent of today's £1. With extra range, navigation became more important, requiring a dedicated navigator. Likewise, bomb aiming became a specialist skill, and the increased complexity of new aircraft types required a second pilot, although later this requirement was satisfied by a flight engineer who managed the aircraft's on-board systems, including the engines. The new aircraft also needed advanced communications equipment, so a further specialisation of wireless operator was required.

The complexity of teamwork in the air was mirrored on the ground. Specialist technicians were need for airframes, engines, radio systems and armament. Backing them up was the need for intelligence, planning, transport, air traffic control (although only at airfields), administration, messing, and a host of other functions. Procurement and supply of equipment had long been a specialist activity in the RAF, managed by the officers of the Supply Branch. The Technical Officer branch was now established with engineering and signals specialisations to manage in-service maintenance of aircraft, their engines, and on-board systems, and also the new radar sites which were rapidly being built as part of the Air Defence of Great Britain – itself a new concept in aerial war. Many of the new airfields for Bomber Command can still be identified simply by driving up the A1 trunk road or taking a train along the East Coast Main Line railway. It was not for the convenience of airmen that these sites were chosen; it was because of the need for a constant supply of the munitions which were to be dropped on the enemy. By the time Jack Mossop had completed his training the supply system was delivering munitions to bomber bases on a daily basis.

The new aircraft being procured were much heavier than previous models. Grass airfields were not always viable, and concrete runways sometimes had to be laid, alongside an increasing infrastructure of bomb dumps, fuel depots, and hangars where unserviceable aircraft could be repaired. Scheduled maintenance was rarely necessary because few aircraft would reach the number of flying hours which would require it, but the tradesmen needed to keep the bombers flying still had to be recruited and trained.

The combined impact of all these factors required significant effort at a time when the RAF was absorbing an unforeseen number of new recruits. By the end of the war in Europe, about 100,000 aircrew had flown in Bomber Command and 55,573 had been killed. As I have already indicated, death can never be far away in this story. About 10 per cent of the fatalities were in accidents, in training and other flying, the remainder were during operations against the enemy. Of those who were flying in Bomber Command at the beginning of the war, 90 per cent had been killed by the end of the war in Europe. The overall loss rate was over 55 per cent; a sacrifice exceeded only by the German submariners in their U-Boats.

The immediate issue in 1939, however, was to establish tactics appropriate to the need. And the need would be based on strategic requirements. It soon became clear that the UK could be isolated from the rest of Europe. The only means, in the short-term at least, of taking the fight to the enemy was through the use of air power. This factor was the main driver behind the strategic decision to launch a bomber offensive. The German people had to be made aware that they had an active and capable enemy, and Germany's ability to support its armies with munitions had to be reduced; these were the twin strategic aims of the bomber offensive. Moreover, Britain's allies and potential allies had also be persuaded that the British were prepared to take the offensive.

As it turned out, by June 1940, the UK was isolated from the rest of Europe. The British Army had escaped by the skin of its teeth at Dunkirk, leaving behind all its equipment. The Royal Navy's traditional strategy of blockade had been thwarted by the vast new tracts of territory held by the enemy, and soon even more so by the deployment of submarines in the Atlantic Ocean. Fighter Command had performed magnificently in the Battle of Britain, achieving local air superiority and thus giving Bomber Command a chance to disrupt the fleet of barges being assembled by the Germans in the Low Countries to convey an invading army across the North Sea. An immediate invasion of England had been averted. But Fighter Command could hold only a shield, not a sword. Churchill summed up the position in a radio broadcast shortly after the Battle of Britain:

The fighters are our salvation, but the bombers alone will provide the means of victory.

Chapter 3

Two Durham Families

Jack and Hilda had been brought up within ten miles of each other, but they did not meet until Jack's part in this story is half-told. The nature of their background was similar, although the Mossops were a larger family. Both families were living in County Durham as the story begins.

The Mossop family was large, with seven children. They took life seriously, to be enjoyed and to be useful. Jack Mossop's father, Joseph Henry Mossop, was born on 6 July 1882 and he married Phyllis Waine a year or so before the start of the First World War. The first of their seven children, Harry, was born in 1914. Joseph fought with the Durham Light Infantry during the war. Family legend has it that his life was saved by a prayer book which stopped a bullet ricocheting off a button on his uniform. He was moving forward into battle and a friend passing in the opposite direction had given him the prayer book, saying that he would need it. A more sceptical generation, familiar with such anecdotes, could be forgiven for asking why the War Office did not simply issue all its soldiers with prayer books, bibles and volumes of Homer; cumulatively, they appear to have saved more lives than the Red Cross. Many families have a similar legend, but at least the Mossops had a damaged button as evidence. Mythical or not, Joseph was back home sometime in 1915 and 1916, because in 1916 Phyllis bore him twins, Joseph and Mary. Another son, William but always called Bill, was also born in 1916. Next came Jack christened John, followed by a daughter, Grace, in 1922. Finally, a seventh child and a fifth boy, Arthur, was born in 1924.

It was a close family, as was often the case in the days before artificial entertainment. Saturday night was for singing songs and playing games around the fireplace, and there was an emphasis on self-education. Spare money was spent on encyclopaedias, and there was a strong desire for advancement.[1] The family home was 13 South View, in the Meadowfield area of the city. South View is still a street in the south suburbs of Durham City, but its houses are of post-war build.

Harry, the eldest child, won a place at Bede College at Durham University, not necessarily to the delight of all his siblings as the family had to sell their piano to support him. He rowed for both his university and for Durham City and he was a member of the Durham crew in the 1936 Durham versus Edinburgh boat race. After graduation with a BA he became senior history master at Consett Grammar School. In 1941, he married Edna Wilson, a school teacher, and they had a child whose name was John, and therefore Jack, but for some reason was called David. The Mossop family seem to have had a penchant for giving gave each other pseudonyms.

Harry, who presumably was once a Henry, applied for and was awarded a cadetship at the Royal Military Academy at Sandhurst. He opted to join his father's regiment, the Durham Light Infantry, on commissioning as an officer. However, it was with the Northamptonshire Regiment that he saw action. He was posted to the Mediterranean theatre where, on 29 July 1943, he was killed during a landing on a Greek island. He was twenty-nine years old.

Of the twins, little is known of Joseph except that, unsurprisingly, he was called Joe. He was born on 16 January 1916 and married a Margaret Sewell. They had a daughter, Jacqueline. He was then called up and served in the Royal Air Force. In the photograph of the four brothers in uniform, Joe is carrying corporal rank stripes. He was posted to the Far East, probably to India but possibly also to Burma. In the unhygienic conditions, inevitable in hastily built camps, he became seriously ill and was repatriated. He survived the war but remained in poor health for the rest of his life.

Joe's twin sister, Mary, trained as a nurse and spent most of the war, including the blitz years, working as a theatre sister in a

London hospital. She was well qualified and became a state examiner, later obtaining a teaching diploma in nursing at Edinburgh University. When the war ended in 1945, Mary joined a world health body and went to the Gambia where she helped to establish a new teaching hospital. When the Gambia achieved independence from the UK in February 1965 Mary returned home and went to live in Liverpool with her twin brother Joe and his wife. By all accounts, Mary was a very competent and highly qualified health professional. She died around 1990, well over seventy years of age.

The next boy, William Mossop was, of course, always called Bill. There is a newspaper cutting containing a photograph of the County of Durham school rugby team which played against a Northumberland County school team in the 1931/32 season. Bill and Jack were both in the team and Jack later played for Durham City Rugby Club. Bill joined the RAF in 1936 when he was only eighteen years old. He qualified as an air gunner, and he first flew on operations in Bristol Blenheim night fighters. By 1942 he had converted to Wellington bombers and was posted to an operational squadron, either No. 425 or No. 426 at RAF Dishforth in Yorkshire. It was at Dishforth that Bill Mossop was fatally injured on 31 January 1943, when a Wellington in which he was the tail gunner failed to take off on a bombing raid, crashing on the end of the runway. He died in Harrogate Hospital at the age of twenty-four.

Jack, whose given name was John but naturally was called Jack from birth, was the fifth of the Mossop siblings, born on 17 April 1920. It is his story which we will use to illustrate the aim and the might of the Allied bombing offensive in the European theatre of the Second World War, and the nature of courtship and marriage during that uncertain time.

The sixth Mossop sibling, Grace, was born on 7 February 1922. As the youngest girl, she was somewhat protected by her older brothers and sisters, which may be why she joined the Women's Auxiliary Air Force, the WAAFs. She served in the WAAF as a VIP driver throughout most of the war. She met her husband Edward Fawcett, obviously called Ted, early in the war, but after being evacuated through Dunkirk Ted was on war duty overseas, mostly in Africa, for the remainder of the war. He finally returned home in 1945, and he married Grace in Durham on 28 February 1946. They lived in Hull for some time, and later in Wetherby. When Ted died in 1997 Grace went to live close to their daughter in Colchester. She died on 31 March 2007.

The youngest of the seven siblings was Arthur, who was called up at the end of the war and served in the Royal Army Pay Corps. After the war he qualified as an accountant and worked in that profession for many years, becoming a director of the textile company Courtaulds.

In 1940, Jack Mossop was twenty years old and a printer by trade, working as a monotype keyboard operator for a local newspaper, *The Durham Advertiser*. However, when still eighteen, rather than wait for the inevitable conscription papers, Jack had volunteered to join the Royal Air Force Volunteer Reserve (RAFVR). Needless to say, the RAFVR was, by then, fully deployed on a wartime basis. Jack attended an Aircrew Selection Board at RAF Watton early in 1940 where he was judged fit for aircrew duties. Then, on 4 March 1940, he was called forward to No. 2 Reception Centre at RAF Cardington. The terms of his engagement were 'D of PE' – Duration of the Present Emergency, which meant until the war was over, whenever that might be. His physical appearance was described on his service record sheet, Form 543:

Height:	5 feet 10½ inches
Chest:	34¾ inches
Colour of Hair:	light brown
Colour of eyes:	grey
Marks, scars etc:	scar on right cheek

The scar on his check could have been a result of rugby injury. More interesting is the record of grey eyes. Those who knew him later saw in his eyes a natural authority which was based on his ability and an inner confidence, but having grey eyes would not seem to have been the cause of this authority as his family saw him as having blue eyes.

The second protagonist in this story is, of course, Hilda Charlton, my mother. Her father, Bill Charlton, was by profession what we would now call a technician, although his occupation is recorded as engineer on his daughters' birth certificates. For many years he worked in the Armstrong factory along the Scotswood Road in Newcastle upon Tyne. During the First World War he had served briefly in the Royal Navy, but before his ship saw action he had been recalled to work in the armament industry. Armstrong was a major supplier of essential munitions to the British Army and the Royal Navy in both world wars. Bill's wife was a milliner, born Ethel Laidler, the daughter of Frederick Charles Laidler, a cabinet maker who had worked for some time on an estate close to Lanchester, a village about five miles north of Durham City. As a cabinet maker he was probably employed to make fixed fittings in the big house. The Laidlers were married at Lanchester on Christmas Day, 25 December 1887, an unusual date for a wedding, but it would have avoided the loss of a day's wages. Their daughter, also named Ethel, was born in Aberdeen, where Frederick had gone temporarily to work.

Just as John Mossop was always called Jack, so was William Charlton always called Bill, at least until another Bill came a long and re-named him Pops, a much easier name to say for a two-year old. My grandfather remained Pops for the rest of his life. He was born on 24 February 1891 at 25 Clyde Street, Wallsend, on Tyneside. His father was William Thomas Charlton – there had always been a Bill in the family.

By 1904 the family had moved to 81 Denmark Street in the Heaton district of Newcastle upon Tyne. After their marriage, Bill and Ethel Charlton lived in the Jesmond district of Newcastle. When Ethel's health began to suffer her doctor suggested that they should move to the countryside where the air would be cleaner. Pops then took a job as a surface engineer in a coalmine in the village of Medomsley in Co. Durham, some four miles from the steel town of Consett, and about six miles from Lanchester where Ethel's mother lived. There was accommodation linked to the job, and the family lived in Stags Head Cottage, which had once been a public house. The cottage is still there, although it is no longer in the shadow of the Derwent Colliery, which closed in the 1960s.

15

They had two daughters, Ethel and Hilda. Ethel joined the Women's Royal Naval Service (the WRENS) for the duration of the war. Hilda became a shorthand typist working for a timber importing company in Newcastle. Timber was an essential war commodity and the documents she handled were classified secret.

Chapter 4

Training

His 1944 diary carries compelling evidence of Jack Mossop's contribution to the air campaign but, as any airman would confirm, success in air battle depends on training as well as the personal qualities of ability and bravery.

Situated a few miles from Bedford, RAF Cardington was a well established RAF base, with a large airfield, famous for being the home base of the ill-fated R101 airship. One of its functions in 1940 was to induct new recruits into the service. When Jack Mossop reported to No. 2 Recruit Centre on 4 March 1940, it was probably the furthest south he had been. He was at Cardington for only two weeks, during which he would have been issued with the standard items of uniform, taught something about how the RAF worked and, most importantly, how to march and to salute. He was also allocated his service number: 954264. Further basic training was provided over the next few months, interspersed with periods of leave. This was a time of the great expansion of the RAF. John Terraine[1] records that on 3 September 1939 the strength of the RAF was 175,692. By September 1940 it had risen to 437,473, and a year later it was approaching a million. The expansion in personnel was mirrored in matériel. New aircraft were being delivered an increasing rate, although not as fast as the RAF would have liked, and new airfields had to be constructed for their bases. Inevitably there was bunching in the training process, and some waiting around. It was not until 25 October 1940, six months after he was enrolled, that Jack Mossop began serious training in the art and science of air warfare.

17

At that time the RAF was struggling to come to terms with the concept and practicalities of large multi-crewed bomber aircraft. A few years previously, in 1937, the RAF acknowledged only one professional category of aircrew, that of pilot. Volunteers were called for when an observer was required, and when the aircraft mounted a gun for self defence either the observer was expected to fire it, or an armament technician would 'volunteer'. Navigation was seen as the pilot's job, although when an observer was carried he might navigate. However, the anticipated realities of operating the new large bombers then in production led to the introduction early in 1938 of a 10-week course to train specialist navigators. It was soon found that in addition to pilots and nav-igators, a bomber crew required specialists in bomb-aiming, radio communications, and air gunnery. Moreover, when four-engined bombers arrived, they needed a specialist flight engineer to work with the pilot in managing the engines and other aircraft systems. Aircrew also had to be able to take over other duties should they take casualties during an operation. Much later, in 1944, Jack Mossop was able to merge his disciplined knowledge covering all aspects of aviation other than actually flying the aircraft. But he had a long road to follow before he became a part of a specialised Pathfinder crew.

The need for trained personnel was not confined to on-board activities. The planning of operations had to consider all the dis-ciplines required in flight to ensure that everyone knew what they were expected to do on a mission. The planners at Command, Group, and Station level were mostly aircrew on ground tours of duty, but some were those who were medically or otherwise unfit for aircrew duties. Ancillary roles such as intelligence officers, supply specialists, air traffic controllers, administrators, caterers, and drivers, were often filled by members of the Women's Auxiliary Air Force (WAAF). The chain of radar and fighter control units, which protected the country from air attack, was also often manned by women. In addition, the RAF was recruit-ing engineers and technicians in large numbers to service the new aircraft, which were much more complex than previous types. A crucial decision had been taken by the Air Force Board early in 1939 to separate the functions of Training Command into two commands: Flying Training Command and Technical Training Command.

The most significant training requirement, with the longest courses, was for pilots. Fortunately, an agreement signed in 1939 with the governments of Canada, Australia, and South Africa had led to what has been described as 'one of the most brilliant pieces of imaginative organisation ever conceived'[2] would provide the aircrew needed for the bomber offensive, which as we shall see, was crucial to the Western Allies' strategy in the war against Germany. The Empire Air Training Scheme, later called the British Commonwealth Air Training Plan, would eventually have over 300 flying training schools, of which around 150 were in the UK, 90 in Canada, about 25 each in Australia and South Africa, and around 35 spread between Southern Rhodesia, India, New Zealand, Bahamas, various Middle Eastern countries and the USA. Many died during their training. To take one example, at Montgomery Alabama, the Commonwealth War Graves Commission maintains a memorial to the seventy-eight officers and other ranks of the RAF who are buried in Oakwood Cemetery. Similar loss rates were experienced at the many other flying schools in the scheme, but the supply of aircrew, particularly pilots, from these schools was sufficient to sustain the air campaign though 1943 and 1944, and into 1945. Jack Mossop would see the benefits of this very successful training scheme in his second and third tours, during which his crew was skippered by a Canadian pilot who had been trained in Canada under the Commonwealth training scheme. In 1941, however, the shortage of new aircraft expected off the productions lines actually led to a surplus of aircrew.

Back in April 1940, however, Jack had himself to be trained in the art of military communications, known generally as signals. First he was posted on 16 July 1940 to No. 3 Electrical and Wireless School at Compton Basset, where he learnt basic techniques, and then on 25 October to No. 2 Electrical and Signals School at Yatesbury, where he learnt about airborne signals techniques. Compton Basset and Yatesbury, both about fifteen miles south-west of Swindon, were the heart of the RAF's highly complex wireless and signals training activity.

Radio equipment had been installed in aircraft almost as soon as wireless communication was invented. Both telephony and telegraphy were used, but in Bomber Command voice messages were mostly limited to communications with airfields for local air traffic purposes. Messages to and from bomber aircraft on bombing operations were conducted using Morse code. The first skill required of a wireless operator was therefore competence in the Morse code. The wireless equipment in the 1940s was reasonably reliable, but its use required an understanding of radio frequency management and a sensitive approach in tuning both the transmitter and the receiver. Tuning was thus the second skill which Jack required. A third skill was traffic management. Incoming messages have to be written down and passed to the intended recipient; not a difficult task, but one which requires an organised approach. Mostly the bomber crews would fly in radio silence, at least on the outbound leg of a raid, to avoid warning the enemy of their presence.

It was at Yatesbury that Jack first flew. The course included about four hours flying in Dominie Mk1 aircraft. The de Havilland Dominie, a two engined biplane, was a version of the de Havilland Dragon which had, for over ten years, been the mainstay of civilian airline flying in UK. It was fitted with a direction-finding loop aerial above the fuselage, which contained a five or six seat airborne classroom. Jack was issued with an Observer's and Air Gunner's Flying Log Book (Form 1767) in which he would now record all his time in the air. The signals schools employed civilian pilots. Jack's first two flights were piloted by Mr Beck on 6 November 1940. In the early afternoon the class practised receiver tuning for one hour, landing at 15.25. Twenty minutes later he was airborne again to practise transmitter tuning, again for about an hour. The following week, on 13 November, Mr Howman was the pilot while the class worked on log keeping, an essential part of signals traffic management and one at which Jack became scrupulous. And then on 18 November, Mr Penrose was the pilot in a one hour flight, during which the mysteries of back-tuning were explored.

Jack finished his signals training at Yatesbury on 11 December 1940 having achieved a Morse speed of eighteen words per minute, duly certified on page 1 of his log book, and signed by Squadron Leader John. The next stage in his training would be noisier. On 23 December he reported to No. 9 Bombing and Gunnery School at Penrhos.

If his wireless training was to put him in the deep south of England, Jack's gunnery training was equally far west. Penrhos is on the south side of the Lleyn Peninsula in north-west Wales. There was no hanging around here. In a period of six weeks, which included Christmas and New Year, Jack qualified as an air gunner. He was airborne for a total of sixteen hours and thirty minutes; eleven flights in Whitley aircraft, and three in Battle aircraft. Here, the pilots were all experienced RAF people; two of them, by their names, were Polish. The duration of each flight was about one hour.

The Armstrong Whitworth Whitley was still, at that time, a front-line bomber, although the type would be taken out of Bomber Command's order of battle early in 1942. It first entered service in 1937, and Whitley Mk III aircraft took part in the first operation of the war when, on 3 September 1939, 51 and 58 Squadrons were detailed to drop propaganda pamphlets over France and the Low Countries. 'Bomber' Harris, later to be demonised as the Commander-in-Chief of Bomber Command, thought this a questionable use of resources, and he later expressed the view that the only thing achieved was 'largely to supply the Continent's requirements of toilet paper for the five long years of war'[3] More usefully, it was a Whitley of 102 Squadron which Leonard Cheshire flew when he won an immediate DSO for gallantry during a raid on Cologne on 12 November 1940. We will meet Cheshire again in this story.

About the Fairey Battle, there is little to say. A single engined light bomber with a fixed gun firing forward and a trainable gun aft, it had been out-gunned during the German attack on the low countries early in 1940. History remembers the type from the brave attack on the Maastricht bridges on 10 May 1940. When volunteers were called for to attack the bridges, in a last ditch attempt to halt the German advance, all surviving members of 12 Squadron stepped forward. Six crews took off, two were shot down and captured, three perished over the target area, and one returned to base but crashed on landing with only one survivor. One of the pilots, Flying Officer Garland, and Sergeant Gray (his observer) both received posthumous VCs. As John Terraine puts

21

it, 'for one or other of the inscrutable reasons which govern these matters, Leading Aircraftman Reynolds, the "part-time air gunner", received no reward'[4]

As a keen airman, Jack Mossop would certainly have been aware of the 12 Squadron heroics, and he may have pondered the unremarked fate of Leading Aircraftman Reynolds. But more likely he was enjoying himself over the firing ranges of the Lleyn Peninsula. At the age of twenty, like most young men he would have relished the chance to fire 2,600 rounds from the .303 calibre guns at targets which did not fight back. He had started with 423 rounds on a ground range at 200 and 400 yards, gaining a 'pass' score. Then, firing 800 rounds air-to-air he scored a hit rate of 2.5 per cent using a beam-mounted gun, 3.9 per cent of 1,000 rounds with another beam gun, 3.5 per cent of 400 free firing against a quartering target, and 1.8 per cent of 600 rounds from an under-tail position. The percentage figures seem small, but they were sufficient to earn a pass from the tutors. In reality, air-to-air gunnery is beset with so many variables that only a small proportion of bullets would hit the target, no matter how expert the gunner. Most successful bomber on fighter engagements during operations occurred when the two aircraft were very close to each other.

Overall, Jack scored 66 per cent on the course. The results were recorded in Jack's log book, where the chief instructor, a wing commander with an illegible signature, added the remark 'Should make a sound air gunner'. Perhaps the wing commander had a droll sense of humour.

It is one thing to be able to fire aircraft guns, and to understand the theory and practice of airborne wireless telegraphy. It is another to be able to use these skills in battle. On 1 February 1941, Jack was posted to RAF Cottesmore, in Rutland, where he would stay until June as a trainee at No. 14 Operational Training Unit (OTU). The training syllabus fell into three phases.

First, in 'B' Flight of 14 OTU, he had reinforcement of his basic training as a wireless telegraphy operator, flying initially in Hampden aircraft. The eleven flights in this phase of training were typically one hour in duration and provided familiarity with the aircraft type in which Jack would soon go to war. The tasks allocated were mostly routine: frequency changing, direction finding to base, and weather reports. The syllabus included classroom sessions covering crew cooperation as well as the theory and practice of radio communication. Jack would, for the first time, be able to talk with aircrew who had completed a tour of duty and were now instructing others. This phase of training lasted just over two weeks.

On 21 April, Jack moved into the second phase. This was more intensive, but it was still restricted to the wireless operator role. The flying element of the syllabus took place in Anson aircraft. Based on the Avro 652 six-passenger commercial aircraft, the Anson had been introduced to the RAF in 1936 for armed recon-naissance duties, but it was also used for training and as a communications aircraft; in RAF parlance a communications aircraft is one which is used to move people around, such a senior officers. Like all the aircraft types which the aircrew liked, the Anson had an affectionate nickname: in this case, Faithful Annie. Perhaps the Anson's most significant contribution was its extensive use in the Commonwealth Air Training Plan. Over 10,000 Anson aircraft were built, nearly 3,000 of them in Canada. The type was not officially retired from the RAF until 1968, by which time it had certainly lived up to its nickname. I can recall having an air experience flight in an Anson as a cadet in 1962.

Jack flew eighteen times in Ansons at 14 OTU, two of them at night. His log book contains entries such as:

Working Base and loop beacon; Contact with base -MTBs; Set temp u/s – remedied fault and obtained QDMs from no 2 D/F;Night – Base – Sealand and Heston M/F

And there is one which has chilling link to a future flight:

Base a/c & d/f – fixes from Bircham Newton and Heston M/F

Jack was nearly killed at Bircham Newton, as we will see later. For the moment his total of forty hours in Ansons completed the second phase of operational training. For the third phase of training Jack moved to 'A' Flight of 14 OTU. All his training flights were now in Hampden aircraft, and the syllabus was no longer restricted to the wireless operator role; ten of the thirty-

23

one airborne training sessions were in the air gunner role. General airmanship issues were covered, including how to abandon the aircraft. Jack's signature appears in his log book under the words:

> Certified that I have carried out practices in 'abandonment of Hampden aircraft' and parachute and dinghy.

Curiously, he was not required to sign a similar declaration for other types in which he would fly operationally.

Later in the war, bomber crews were formed as early as possible in the induction and training period as it was realised that the better they knew each other, the more effective they were in battle. Modern theories on team-building sometimes forget such simplicities. The RAF crew-making approach evolved to become both highly successful, and alarmingly simple. New aircrew mixed informally, often in a hangar with a barrel of beer available, with those being re-roled and they sorted themselves into crews. They were then posted as crews and kept together as much as possible. In 1941, however, aircrew were still being posted individually. It must have been through coincidence that Sergeant Latty, the pilot on the Hampden during Jack's first flight in 'A' Flight at 14 OTU, was posted to 49 Squadron at about the same time as Jack; they would fly together on two operations early in July.

The training was now intensive. Jack flew thirty-three times between 8 May and 16 June, clocking up 56 hours and 55 minutes of flying time. But eventually the preparation was over. On 1 June 1941, the Officer Commanding Training Wing of 14 OTU, another wing commander with an indecipherable signature, signed a 'Summary of Flying and Assessments' form which was pasted into Jack's flying log. Jack was assessed as 'above average' in the two roles of Signals and Air Gunnery. He was posted to 49 Squadron at RAF Scampton on 30 June 1941, presumably after taking some leave. He was twenty-one years old and had been in the RAFVR for fifteen months. He now faced the biggest challenge in his life.

24

Chapter 5

The War in 1941

While Jack went through the necessary preparation, a real war as being fought. Germany had occupied Holland, Belgium and most of France, and Britain was ready to defend itself against a German invasion. Since the evacuation of the British Army from Dunkirk in May 1940, the RAF's priorities had been set by the enemy, and the most important was to prevent an invasion. Fortunately, the German Air Force, the *Luftwaffe*, had not been created in a manner which would allow it to take up a strategic role. It was a very competent tactical air force whose role was to support Army operations. To be sure, the *Luftwaffe* had some aircraft, the Messerschmitt 109 being perhaps the prime example, which could outfight any other equivalent aircraft type of the day. But its command structure was not set up for a strategic campaign, and German factories were never asked to produce the heavy types of bomber which became the backbone of Bomber Command. When Hitler realised that he could command neither the airspace nor the sea around the British Isles, he turned his attention away. His strategy now was to isolate the UK while the German Army, with the *Luftwaffe* in support, conquered one European country after another, and so far the strategy had been mostly successful. He had expected the UK to surrender, but the Battle of Britain had revealed the limits of the *Luftwaffe*. Furthermore, Germany's ally, Italy, had suffered a major setback when the British Fleet Air Arm destroyed its navy at Taranto. Two battleships were sunk, another severely damaged, and two cruisers were left badly listing. The balance of naval power in the Mediterranean shifted critically – a demonstration of the potential of air power to destroy strategic targets through concentration of effort. The lesson was not lost on the fast growing RAF.

On the other hand, the destruction of Coventry Cathedral by the *Luftwaffe* on 14 November showed what mass bombing could achieve. Whatever qualms might arise after the war over the RAF's bombing of German cities, in 1940 there was effectively no doubt amongst the civilian population of Britain, nor in its government, and certainly not in its air force, that the cities of Germany had to be attacked if the war was to be won. The London blitz in the first part of 1941 strongly reinforced this view. When extended into action, strategic air power has the unfortunate distinction of causing civilian casualties, often at a higher rate than the actual combatants. This distinction remained true throughout the Second World War, and potentially even more so, although thankfully not tested, in the subsequent Cold War.

During 1941 the RAF set about the job of creating in Bomber Command a strategic air capability. In his book *Bomber Offensive*,[1] Marshal of the Royal Air Force Sir Arthur Harris, whilst acknowledging that occupation of enemy territory would always require ground forces, explains that no other country had, at that time, tried to use an air force to fight a war, and effectively to win a war. As already noted, the French saw bombers as a type of long-range artillery and the *Luftwaffe* existed entirely to support the German Army, whilst the Russians seem never to have even considered strategic bombing. Apart from their attack on Pearl Harbor, which in any case was a naval battle, the Japanese seem to have seen their air force as a junior partner to the army. Only the British had used air power as a strategic force, most notably in Iraq in the 1920s, but never on the scale now contemplated.

Chapter 6

The First Tour

His service record shows that Jack was initially posted to RAF Scampton to join 144 Squadron, on 25 June 1941. However, within five days of arrival the posting was changed, and he joined 49 Squadron, which was also at Scampton. Both squadrons flew Hampden bombers, and both had been blooded in the first bombing operations of the war. On 29 September 1939, 144 Squadron had lost all five aircraft to enemy fighters in an attempt to bomb German destroyers near Heligoland,[1] whilst 49 Squadron had taken part in the very first operation on the day that war was declared.

In accordance with a regulation brought in the previous year, Jack was promoted to Temporary Sergeant when he reported for operational duties. As explained in Chapter 4, the definition of aircrew roles had only recently been agreed. Previously air gunners and wireless operators were drawn from any applicable ground trade discipline, so airmen fitters could suddenly find themselves flying operationally as volunteers with little additional training, and little more pay. With trained professionals now in each role, the value of crew cooperation had been realised, and by June 1941 the benefits of keeping crews together had been accepted.

No. 49 Squadron[2] was one of the RAF's most famous, and its reputation had already been enhanced by the first Victoria Cross awarded to a Bomber Command pilot. Flight Lieutenant Learoyd had displayed the high level of valour required for the UK's highest military honour during a raid on the night of 12 August 1940 in which delayed action bombs were dropped on an aqueduct in the Dortmund-Ems canal. The squadron's badge features a greyhound courant, indicative of speed, and its motto was Cave Canem, 'Beware of the dog'; its teeth were certainly in action that night as they would be during the next six months.

The squadron was later to operate in Kenya during the Mau Mau uprising and it took part in the UK nuclear bomb trials at Christmas Island in 1956/57, during which a 49 Squadron aircraft dropped the first British hydrogen bomb. The squadron finally disbanded on 1 May 1965 when the RAF's fleet of Valiant bombers was grounded due to metal fatigue.

RAF Scampton is probably the most well known of all Bomber Command stations. It was first opened in 1916, when it was known as Brattleby. Four miles north of Lincoln, it was the first of a number of airfields on the Lincoln Ridge which runs on the west side of the A15 road. By 1917 its name had changed to Scampton, and it accommodated a home defence squadron flying FE 2b two-seater fighters. The station was closed in 1920, but abandoned First World War landing grounds were the first to be considered when the RAF started to expand around 1930. The site was extended to accommodate four large Type C hangars and substantial brick-built operations and administration buildings. The large weapons stores were put well away on the east side of the base. The work was completed in 1937, but there were two squadrons in residence by 1936. No. 9 Squadron flew Handley Page Heyfords, the last of the RAF's biplane bombers, and No. 214 flew Vickers Virginias.

The Virginias were soon taken away as trainers for parachute jumping; about the only role they could fill. Having first seen RAF service in 1924 they were no longer viable as operational aircraft. However, they were replaced by another non-viable type, the Handley Page Harrow, a monoplane bomber converted from a troop carrier. The Harrow did, however, achieve some fame when two of them evacuated wounded soldiers from Arnhem in September 1944. No. 214 Squadron was transferred from Scampton in April 1937.

The seemingly constant relocation and re-equipping of squadrons in the three years before the Second World War started is evidence, not of confusion and lack of control, but rather of the urgent need to prepare for a war which had not been properly anticipated. The RAF's own history of Scampton contains a passage which well illustrates the impact of necessary reorganisation and re-equipment during the final few years of peace:

In June, 'C' Flight of No. 9 Squadron became the reformed No. 148 Squadron, flying Audax biplanes for two months while awaiting Wellesley monoplanes. In March 1938, the recently formed No. 5 Group was given bomber stations in Lincolnshire so Nos. 9 and 148 Squadrons moved south to No. 3 Group's new station at Stradishall. Their place was taken by Nos. 49 and 83 Squadrons, ex-Worthy Down and Turnhouse respectively. Both surrendered their Hawker Hinds for Handley Page Hampdens later in the year.

The youngest recipient of the Victoria Cross during the Second World War flew from Scampton. Sergeant John Hannah was a wireless operator/air gunner in a No. 83 Squadron Hampden, which was set on fire by a direct flak hit in the bomb-bay while attacking invasion barges on 15 September 1940. Sergeant Hannah could have baled out but he stayed and fought the fire, which enabled his Canadian pilot to fly the crippled machine back to Scampton. One of the pilots in 83 Squadron at that time was Flying Officer Guy Gibson who won perhaps the most celebrated VC of all time when he returned to Scampton as a wing commander to lead No. 617 Squadron in the famous raid on the Ruhr dams with Barnes Wallis's rotating mine.

No. 49 Squadron had been the first squadron to be equipped with Handley-Page Hampden aircraft.[3] The Hampden was the third of three types of two-engined bomber introduced by the RAF in the three years prior to the outbreak of hostilities in 1939, the other two being the Vickers Wellington and the Armstrong Whitworth Whitley. All three types were initially used in the daylight bombing role, for which the Hampden was particularly inadequate. The Wellington and the Whitley had powered gun turrets which provided some degree of self-defence against enemy fighters, but the Hampden's guns had to be trained by hand, apart from one fixed gun mounted above the cockpit which was fired by the pilot. In the nose of the aircraft there was a dismountable gun which was stowed on the starboard side of the fuselage when not needed for combat. There were also two rear-facing guns. These were mounted above and below the wireless operator's seat which was a few feet behind the pilot. The forward firing guns were of little value in air combat, and the rearward facing guns had blind spots where the gunners could not see attacking aircraft. Furthermore, there were restrictions on their arc of fire, to avoid hitting parts of the aircraft. Another deficiency was the poor crew accommodation which was both cramped and unheated. The navigator's position was in a cockpit in front of and below the pilot's cockpit. From that position, the navigator, who also acted as the bomb-aimer, could see the ground easily. His cockpit mounted navigation instruments on the port side and bomb-aiming, and bomb release equipment on the starboard side. When 'Bomber' Harris took command of No. 5 Group in 1939, he considered the Hampden:

> ...an aircraft which failed to meet many requirements of the normal specifications, especially with regard to comfort for the crew... .[4]

His main complaint was over the sparse level of crew comfort in the Hampden which could induce fatigue, potentially fatal, especially if enemy fighters were around. The human body does not work too well in cramped and cold conditions. These deficiencies led to Bomber Command's Hampden fleet being grounded for a period in 1940. Some improvements to the guns were made, but by the time Jack joined 49 Squadron the Hampdens were supposedly used in night operations only, when no opposition was expected.

The Hampden did, however, have some good attributes. Its long tapered fuselage, which gave it the nickname Flying Panhandle, provided good manoeuvrability, and it was fast, with a maximum speed of 254 mph at 13,800 feet. The Wellington, although probably a better aircraft all round, could reach only 235 mph at 15,500 feet. Despite its vulnerability and its crew discomfort, the Hampden could be an effective bomber, able to carry 2,000lb of bombs a distance of 1,885 miles, or 4,00lb of bombs a distance of 1,200 miles.

Guy Gibson had flown a Hampden in the first raid of the war, when he was with 83 Squadron. In the evening of the day on which Neville Chamberlain announced that Great Britain was at war with Germany, 3 September 1939, eighteen Hampdens were sent to bomb German warships in the Schillig Roads of Wilhemshaven. No. 49 Squadron contributed aircraft to the raid. By the time they reached the target areas it was getting dark and no warships could be found. As Gibson's biographer puts it, the only real achievement of the raid was that all the aircraft returned safely to Scampton.[5] The inadequacies of the Hampden as a strategic bomber were soon to be apparent, but they did play a significant role in the Battle of Britain, bombing the fleets of sea-going barges which the Germans were assembling in Belgian and Dutch ports preparatory to an invasion of England.

The wireless equipment which Jack Mossop was to operate during his first tour was relatively simple when compared with the equipment which would be available later in his career. In his compartment in a Hampden he had a transmitter Type T 1083 and a receiver Type R1082. The radios worked in the high frequency band (3 to 30 MHz) which allowed long range communication beyond the horizon but at the risk of interference from the effects of weather. Tuning was critical and required considerable skill. The means of modulating the radio wave was through a transmitter key using Morse code. There were two types of aerial. A screened loop aerial allowed the operator to determine the direction of a radio signal. This assisted navigation, particularly when returning to base; by homing on a continuous signal from their home airfield they could find their way back. To send and receive messages, however, a larger aerial was required. This took the form of a long stainless steel wire trailed behind the aircraft. When not in use the aerial wire was wound on a winch. In a Hampden, Jack would have the controls for the Aerial Winch Type 5. He would also have to mind an 80 watt DC motor-generator which produced the power for the radio transmitter. Power for the radio receiver came from a 4.2 volt 20 ampere-hour accumulator, for which there was a reserve accumulator.

Sixty-five years on, the radio fit in Hampdens seems archaic, particularly when the need for an operator to tune both transmitters and receivers by hand is taken into account. But the science of ground to air wireless and radio telephony was advancing rapidly, spurred on by the needs of an increasingly technological conflict. One of the themes of this story is how technology advanced at an enhanced rate through the war years, particularly in the field of engineering which is now known as electronics.

Jack Mossop was now ready to join the fray. He had learned much by then about bombing tactics and the capabilities of the aircraft in which he was about to fight. He had been trained to operate efficiently, but survival depended on experience as well as knowledge. He would, of course, lean on the experience of others longer in the fray, but even experienced crews did not live long. In describing his feelings towards the end of his first tour, Guy Gibson wrote:

And so I went to bed. I was the last one left, the last one out of a bunch of boys who belonged to 83 Squadron at the beginning of the war...As I lay in bed thinking, I knew I was lucky to survive, but it would come to me any day now. We would go on and on until the whole squadron was wiped out, then there would be new boys to carry out our traditions, new squadrons, new gadgets, and new ground crews to crack jokes as we took to the air...I did not see any point in living.[6]

Guy Gibson's account in *Enemy Coast Ahead* of the early stage of the bombing campaign gives a vivid and believable picture of the peculiar circumstances of bomber crews. A group of people, among whom a twenty-three year old would be considered old, who one night could enjoy a party in the mess, or an evening at the theatre, or in the pubs in the nearest town, could, the next night, be fighting for their lives in a damaged bomber hardly able to stay airborne. Statistically, only half of them were likely to survive a full tour, but they would not have known that.

To be detailed for an operation was, of course, the sole purpose of aircrew; the focus of their training. But it had soon been recognised that it was impossible to maintain effectiveness if aircrew were detailed for one operation after another with no end in sight. The length of a tour of operational duty had therefore been set for thirty operations. Everyone on an operational tour knew how

32

many 'ops' he had been on, and perhaps of more immediate concern, how many more he had to do. The golden figure of thirty was every man's goal. Few would rationalise the figure as a measure of risk, but the risk of being shot down, with the possible consequences of death, wounding, or become a prisoner of war, increased with every operation. Risk has two dimensions: the harm caused when something goes wrong, and exposure, which can be expressed by a number or by time. It is the time dimension which is the more insidious. Some aircrew were lost on their first operation, but any sortie could be their last; it is the time dimension of risk which catches out those who are regularly exposed. Jack was fond of quoting Shakespeare, perhaps to the annoyance of his colleagues, and he might have been aware of these lines which come from *Troilus and Cressida*, that powerful play about another violent war in which the tread of time was the real enemy.

> Time hath, my lord, a wallet at his back
> wherein he puts alms for oblivion,
> a great-sized monster of ingratitudes:
> those scraps are good deeds passed
> which are devoured as fast as they are made,
> forgot as soon as done
> perseverance, dear my lord, keeps honour bright

As is often the case with Shakespeare, he seems to understand the concerns of the twentieth century as easily as of his own. The Trojan War was long and violent. In this speech Achilles uses the imagery of time, slowly collecting its dues, to explain the nature of risk to his colleague, Ulysses. Good deeds accomplished do not necessarily lead to survival, and honour requires that the fight continues. As we have seen, not all risk facing aircrew derived from operations; overall, for every six killed in action, one was killed in training or other accidents. But it was the ratchet-like count of operations which fed the great-sized monster of ingratitude, providing the tempo and regulating an individual's exposure to risk. Recognising this tempo, I will note each increase in alms for oblivion by noting Jack's count of operations, slowly but steadily filling time's wallet.

Jack first experienced operational flying on the day he joined 49

Squadron, 30 June 1941. He was two months short of his twenty-first birthday. Take-off was at 23.10[7] in a Hampden bomber piloted by Sergeant Huggett. The target was to have been Düsseldorf, but a weather forecast led to a change, and they attacked Kiel (Op. 1). The Hampden's tail number was AD896. Two aircraft from Scampton, tail numbers XK336 and AZ558, did not return. Altogether, Bomber Command launched sixty-four sorties that night. Their losses were five aircraft (two Hampdens and three Whitleys) and twenty-three crew (7 per cent of the attacking force). Jack and his comrades had entered the treadmill of risk. Time's wallet began to fill.

For his next two operations Jack joined the crew of Sergeant Latty, who had been on the instructing staff at Cottesmore. On 3 July 1941 they bombed the shipyards at Bremen (Op. 2). The sortie time of this flight was 7 hours and 20 minutes. Other squadrons from Scampton laid mines in the sea around the Friesian Islands. The war in the Atlantic was in a critical phase at this time, and naval targets such as ports and their approaches were given a high priority. Bomber Command launched 163 aircraft on the night of 3 July, targeted at Essen, Bremen, and various aerodromes. Nine (6 per cent) did not return. When daylight raids on 4 July are included, the total losses in the 24-hour period were fifteen aircraft and sixty-six aircrew.[8]

Scampton launched no raid on 4 July, but instead the station had the privilege of a visit by Air Chief Marshal Sir Richard Pierse, who was Air Officer Commanding-in-Chief (AOC.-in-C.) of Bomber Command. He had held this post since October 1940, having previously been Vice-Chief of the Air Staff. These were difficult times for Bomber Command. Following a lengthy debate on the accuracy and effectiveness of the bombing campaign, a conference of navigation officers in May 1941 had concluded that 50 per cent of Bomber Command's bombs were falling in open country.[9] Whilst the War Cabinet was demanding a bombing campaign which would reduce Germany's ability to fight the war through attacks on oil installations and munitions factories, Pierse was reluctantly acknowledging that the only targets which could possibly be attacked with some certainty of accuracy were whole towns. Whether he discussed this gradual change in the bombing policy with the crews at Scampton is not known, but as their operational leader, Pierse would have wished to test their reaction.

Concern over the accuracy of bombing had also reached the War Cabinet in London. Winston Churchill's Scientific Advisor set up a statistical review which was conducted by Mr Butt, who worked in the War Cabinet Secretariat in London. After examining photographs taken during bombing missions, Mr Butt concluded that of those bombers which were recorded as actually attacking the target only one third dropped their bombs within five miles of the target. However, only one third of bombers sent out on a raid actually attacked the target. So, if ninety bombers took off, thirty would attack the target, of which only ten would be within five miles of the target when they dropped their bombs. This was a somewhat disappointing conclusion, which some disputed, but it was consistent with Bomber Command's own findings, and it led to the realisation that getting bombs on target was more a matter of navigation than of bomb-aiming, at least at this stage of the campaign. Later in this story we will look at the various technological advances which were harnessed to overcome this significant deficiency in bombing accuracy evident in 1941.

Meanwhile the bombing continued. The target on 5 July 1941 was Osnabrück (Op. 3), and Jack was again crewed with Sergeant Latty. Bomber Command launched 208 crews that night, of which seventeen (8 per cent) failed to return. The Scampton Operations Record Book records:

Sergeant Latty returned after 40 minutes with starboard engine unserviceable in X3185.

All RAF Units are required by regulation to complete F540, the Operational Record Book (ORB), often called the monthly diary. Operational units were also required to complete F451, a daily summary. Unfortunately there was, during the Second World War, a large variation in the level of detail recorded by the organisations required to maintain Forms 540 and 451. Entries vary from non-existent to lengthy expositions on good or bad fortune. Most ORBs from this period are lodged in the National Archives at Kew and are a valuable source of information for stories such as Jack Mossop's flying career, despite the numerous blank entries. Sometimes, because both the operational squadrons and their parent RAF Stations were required to raise ORBs, it is possible to find two sources of information on flying operations. The converse also applies, and for Jack's next two sorties there is no information from either source. However, his flying log provides some details.

Jack now became a regular member of Sergeant Bunn's crew, as an air gunner, flying in Hampden AD980. On 8 July 1941 they attacked Hamm (Op. 4), not quite in the Ruhr Valley, which would later absorb his energies on several occasions, but close. Two nights later, the target was Cologne (Op. 5); another place Jack would see more of. On 12 July, Jack was listed as the wireless operator as well as an air gunner. The target was Bremen (Op. 6), and the Scampton ORB records that aircraft based at Scampton had to land at Mildenhall, in East Anglia because of bad weather in Lincolnshire. For the operation on 14 July 1941 Sergeant Bunn was replaced by Pilot Officer Harvey for some reason not known. The mission was 'gardening', the code word for sea-mining, on this occasion off Heligoland (Op. 7). The approaches to the North German sea ports of Wilhelmshaven, Bremerhaven, and Hamburg were crucial to the German navy's efforts to disrupt shipping across North Atlantic which in turn was crucial to the survival of Britain. Bomber Command regularly mined the approaches to the naval ports on the North German coast in an attempt to blockade the ports.

Jack flew six more sorties with Sergeant Bunn, all in Hampden AD980. The frequency of missions was relentless. During the three weeks from 16 July to 5 August 1941, they bombed Hamburg (Op. 8), Aachen (Op. 9), Frankfurt (Op. 10), Hanover (Op. 11) and Karlsruhe (Op. 14), and they dropped mines in the sea off Heligoland and in Kiel Bay (Op. 12). They had another mining operation on 2 August but were unable to find the target because of weather conditions (Op.13). It was by no means unusual, but it was still an enormous load for a newly qualified crew. Jack logged twelve operations in July with a total of nearly 93 hours of operations and nearly 6 hours of training and flight testing flying. The average length of an operational sortie, excluding 5 July when they had to return with an unserviceable engine, was just over 6¾ hours. The longest was on 28 July when the mine-laying operation in Kiel (Op. 12) took 8 hours 15 minutes, and this was in one of the least comfortable aircraft ever built. As already noted, the Hampden did not have much in the way of creature comforts.

August provided some relief. A frustrating night on 2 August, when they could not find the target area in a mining operation (Op. 13), was followed on 5 August by a long trip to Karlsruhe (Op. 14) where they at least had the satisfaction of observing fires in the target area. Then for the next two or three weeks, Jack was the wireless operator on a series of night flying exercises and formation practices. He would also have had a week's leave, at last. The unofficial rule, which soon became entrenched as a necessity, was that operational bomber crews should have a week's leave every six weeks. In 1941 the rule was not tight. Jack flew on fourteen operational sorties in twelve weeks before he could take some leave.

Meanwhile, Hitler had played one of his joker cards. The Soviet Union had got what it wanted from its 1939 pact with Germany: most of Poland and the Baltic States. But once he realised that an invasion of Britain was not feasible, Hitler consolidated his hold on his gains in West Europe, and then attacked the Russians. The German invasion had started on 22 June 1941. The fighting ran from the Baltic to the Black Sea, but Hitler's expectation of a quick victory was unfulfilled. The Russians had not learnt from the German tactics in France and Poland, yet a country of her sheer size can afford to lose many hundreds of square miles and many hundreds of soldiers before surrender becomes necessary. In any case, the Red Army was fighting not against subjugation but annihilation. Minsk fell on 30 June, but elsewhere the Germans were suffering heavy casualties. The Russians adopted a scorched earth policy in Ukraine and set Kiev on fire before the Germans took the city on 19 September. The Red Air Force demonstrated expertise in two crucial roles of air warfare: close air support and suppression of key targets behind the enemy's front line. At the end of September a crucial meeting was held in Moscow at which Britain and the USA agreed to supply munitions to Russia. Nevertheless, Moscow was preparing for a siege.

37

On returning from leave, Jack found that he had been transferred to the crew of Pilot Officer Cooke, flying first with him to Frankfurt (Op. 15) on 29 August 1941, then to Cologne (Op. 16) on 31 August, where they could not find the target so they bombed searchlights, and again to Frankfurt (Op. 17) on 12 September. Then they went to Wilhelmshaven (Op. 18) on 15 September and back to Frankfurt (Op. 19) on 28 September, this time having to land at Dishforth in Yorkshire.

Dishforth is much closer to Durham than is Scampton, and it would have been convenient to hitchhike home as he was due some leave. But he had to hand in his parachute and get all his personal kit back in his locker at Scampton. His log shows that Jack was with the crew when they flew the 20 minute hop back to Scampton the next morning. He had no flying duties between 4 and 14 October, and he was at home on leave for most of this time period. As already noted, leave was an important issue for aircrew. All agreed that the introverted and intense atmosphere of a bomber base was not healthy in terms of mental pressure. A bomber base was like a goldfish bowl, with an unending routine of training, practice, briefing, and operations creating recurring sets of activities, all overshadowed by the constant of risk of death and injury in both operations and training. Getting people off the camp was an important way of maintaining sanity, both collective and individual.

As it turned out, Jack was detailed for only two operational sorties in October. On 14th he was with Sergeant Latty's crew, bombing Cologne (Op. 20). They had to land at Martlesham Heath, near Ipswich. On 20 October 1941 he was with Sergeant Watt mining the sea around the Friesland (Op. 21). Jack's flying log contains a rare comment on the mission: 'successful'. But success in dropping mines is relatively easy to achieve. The bombing of specific targets, whether ships or on land, is a very different matter.

At the end of October Jack joined the crew captained by Sergeant Robinson, who was soon to be awarded a commission. The process was now routine and familiar. The targets were selected by the staff at HQ Bomber Command at High Wycombe, using a list of strategic target types drawn up by the Air Staff in London and agreed by the War Cabinet. More prosaically, target selection was also conditioned by the weather. The list of targets would be considered by the staff at the Headquarters of No. 5 Group and allocated to the squadrons. The allocation would be based on the number of aircraft and crews available in each squadron. The allocations stated a specific number of aircraft from each squadron detailed. Bomber squadrons rarely flew all together. The risk of losing a large number of crews from one squadron in a single raid was too high in both operational and human terms. Each squadron had a leader in each flying discipline to ensure that the crews were properly complemented, to define the routes there and back, to arrange the radio call-signs, and to ensure that the right weapons were loaded. By then the aircraft would have been bombed up with the ordnance required by the planners; at this stage of the war the options were usually high explosive bombs or mines, although incendiaries were being considered.

Slowly Jack built his experience, and by the end of November he had twenty-five operations behind him; five more and he would be rested from operational flying. On 3 November 1941 he had flown on an operation with Sergeant Robinson, bombing ship convoys off the Frisians (Op. 22). By the time he was next detailed for an operation, Sergeant Robinson had been awarded a commission and become Pilot Officer Robinson. The task was also something of a change. All Jack's operations so far had involved flying east to reach the target, but on 23 November 1941 the target was Lorient in north-west France, where Admiral Dönitz had set up his U-Boat Headquarters (Op. 23). It was from there that the Germans were sending out instructions to the U-Boat commanders, with devastating effects on the Atlantic convoys which were bringing essential supplies to Britain. Unfortunately, neither 49 Squadron nor the RAF Scampton ORBs record whether this raid was successful. However, Dönitz moved the headquarters to Paris in March 1942, so he may have been concerned by the bombing threat; throughout its occupation the Allies were reluctant to bomb Paris.

The RAF Scampton ORB records an operation on the next day, for which Pilot Officer Robinson's crew was not detailed:

18 aircraft to cause disturbance and the sounding of air raid

warnings in an area in N Germany.

This appears ridiculous, but concern over the lack of accuracy achieved in the dropping of bombs may well have led to a form of psychological warfare as an alternative. More likely it was part of a diversionary measure to mislead ground and airborne defences about the real targets.

Jack was now looking forward to the end of his tour. Thirty operations was the limit, and he had only seven to go. On 26 November 1941 he was over Emden (Op. 24), at the extreme north-west of Germany, bombing harbour facilities. Then on 30 November the target was Hamburg (Op. 25), with a novelty: for the first time they carried a single weapon, a land mine, which would have had a delayed action fuse set to explode at a time when it would cause the maximum disruption.

The next raid was also unusual. The officers detailed to write the ORB entries for both 49 Squadron and RAF Scampton seem to have woken from their slumbers. The target was Aachen (Op. 26), close to the German border with Belgium. The Scampton diary is dry and to the point:

Nazi party HQ – very precise bombing

The 49 Squadron version is more fulsome, and it quotes the debriefing reports from two of the crews:

Attacked last resort, heavy flak in target area. Visibility very poor, thick haze in area of primary target during run-up and bursts reflected on cloud. Large amount of icing cloud experienced.

Attacked as last resort an aerodrome in area of Aachen. Could not locate target owing to limited visibility. Lighting and runways of aerodrome seen, and three bursts resulted.

Perhaps the other crews had arrived earlier and found that the Nazi Party's local HQ already destroyed. The targets of 'last resort' are those which are on the list only to avoid the need to carry bombs home. With enemy fighters aware of the raid, the loss of manoeuvrability when carrying bombs was too much of handicap.

Jack now only had four operations left in his first tour. He nearly did not reach the magic number 30. On 12 December 1941, for the first time, Jack took part in a daylight bombing operation at Cuxhaven (Op. 27). The crew this time was:

Pilot Officer Robinson – pilot

Sergeant Black – navigator

Sergeant Mossop – wireless operator (and air-gunner)

Sergeant Parrot – air gunner

When he got back, Jack added a rare, if terse, comment, additional to the details required by regulations, in the Remarks column of his flying log book:

Operations – Cuxhaven – bombed and strafed aerodrome – strafed town – crashed at Bircham N. Navigator killed.

The RAF Scampton diary provides some details on what had happened:

Daylight raid. At 1550, SOS from Aircraft W. At 1700, information that 'W' had crashed at Bircham Newton, and report that the navigator, Sergeant Black, had died from injuries. The other aircraft from 49 Squadron detailed for this raid, T/L C, abandoned the operation owing to insufficient cloud cover and returned to base.

From this we can assume that only two Scampton aircraft were detailed for this raid, and one had turned back because the clouds did not prevent its presence being noticed from the ground. The other aircraft, tail letter 'W', was that occupied by Pilot Officer Robinson's crew. It crashed on the return leg of the mission. The 49 Squadron diary gives a few more details based on the surviving crew's debrief:

Flying time: 1018 to 1635. Target: naval barracks.
    Attacked alternative aerodrome at Cuxhaven from 100 feet. In face of intense ground opposition 2 aircraft set on fire on ground, possibly 3. Hangar seen to blow up and town

41

machine gunned. Aircraft badly shot up. Hydraulics u/s and Navigator killed by cannon shell. Crash landed at Bircham Newton.

Both Jack Mossop and Sergeant Joseph Price were awarded the Distinguished Flying Medal (DFM) following this raid, and the pilot, Pilot Officer Robinson, was awarded the Distinguished Flying Cross (DFC). Flying over a defended enemy airfield at 100 feet in daylight would significantly increase the normally high risk associated with bomber operations. To make it worse, the defenders seemed to have had only one aircraft on which to concentrate their fire. Some idea of the level of risk can be obtained from the commendations for the DFMs . Of Sergeant Price it was written:[10]

> The objective was attacked from a height of 100 feet in the face of intense opposition from the ground. Sergeant Price used his guns with telling effect and several enemy aircraft were left burning on the ground. His own aircraft sustained much damage as a result of the enemy's cannon fire

Jack's contribution was issued as a press release:

> This airman has taken part in numerous sorties both as Air Gunner and a Wireless Operator. Throughout, he has displayed great skill and efficiency. In December, 1941, he participated in a daylight raid on an enemy aerodrome. During a low level attack on hangars, Sergeant Mossop maintained damaging fire and several Me 109s were destroyed on the ground. His aircraft was repeatedly hit by enemy fire, the Navigator being killed and at least two cannon shells penetrated close to the Wireless Operator's cockpit. During the return journey, Sergeant Mossop carried out his duties so efficiently that his captain was able to reach this country.

Pilot Officer Robinson's DFC citation, which was published in the *London Gazette* on 6 January 1942, provides the best account of this small battle:[11]

> In December 1941 this officer was the pilot of an aircraft which carried out a daring attack on an enemy aerodrome in

daylight. Just before the attack was made, the Perspex of the navigator's cockpit was shattered by a bird, but the attack was pressed home from a height of only 100 feet despite considerable opposition. Bombs were released on a hangar while a number of Messerschmitt 109's on the ground were machine-gunned and set on fire. Pilot Officer Robinson's aircraft was hit by a cannon shell which riddled the navigator's cockpit and so seriously wounded the navigator that he died shortly afterwards. The aircraft sustained other damage, and the inter-communication and hydraulic systems were put out of action; the pilot's instrument panel was also damaged. Pilot Officer Robinson set course for this country and meanwhile the rear gunner tended the badly wounded navigator and beat out flames from his burning clothing. Over coming many difficulties, Pilot Officer Robinson flew back to an aerodrome in this country where he made a perfect landing with the undercarriage retracted. This officer has completed 24 operational missions over enemy country and has also shown high courage and great devotion to duty.

There is no evidence to suggest that any other aircraft attacked Cuxhaven aerodrome. The only other Scampton aircraft involved returned because of a lack of cloud cover, presumably before reaching either of the two targets. And there is no information to explain why the naval barracks were not attacked, or even why they were the primary target. The destruction of several Me109 fighter aircraft would be a better gain than a few holes knocked through the walls of a barrack building. The Me109 was the *Luftwaffe*'s best fighter, at least equal to the RAF's Spitfire and in many ways better. Perhaps the crew of the only Hampden to reach Cuxhaven decided themselves that the aerodrome was a more valuable target. But in retrospect, it seems astonishing that two aircraft not designed for the ground attack role were sent on a raid against a well defended aerodrome.

The last sentence of the press release suggests that Jack effectively took over the navigation role on the return journey while also sending radio messages to warn Scampton that they would most likely have to crash land at the first airfield they could reach. Scampton is virtually due west of Cuxhaven, but Bircham

Newton, some thirty miles south of the direct track, was the first airfield they could reach, still seventy miles from Scampton. If they could achieve the Hampden's maximum speed of 254 mph, which seems unlikely, they would have had to remain airborne for about another twenty minutes to reach Scampton. Jack was probably calling the shots while Pilot Officer Robinson struggled with the controls; it was a close call, but the diversion to Bircham Newton may have saved their lives.

Perhaps fortunately for this narrative, Jack was not detailed for another daylight operation until 1944 when he was involved in support for the Normandy landings. His DFM was gazetted on 13 February 1942, a fact duly entered into his record of service (Form 543) maintained by the RAF Records Office at Innsworth. HM The King presented the medal to Jack on 19 May 1942, at Buckingham Palace. Jack's parents travelled to London to attend the investiture. Sometime later, in fact well over a year later, the gratuity of £30 which comes with the award of a DFM was authorised in a letter to Lloyds Bank dated 9 October 1943. £30 was quite a large sum in 1943, equivalent to about £900 in 2006. Curiously, as Jack would find out, commissioned officers who were awarded the DFC received no gratuity; instead, they received a letter thanking them for their contribution to the RAF Benevolent Fund.

In the meantime, there was a tour to complete. Sergeant Parrot took the place of the deceased Sergeant Black in the crew, but their next flight was not until after Christmas. It is not clear whether the suspension of operations over the Christmas period was intended. There are two entries in the Scampton ORB for 24 December:

10.25: Informed 'Bomber Command stand down tonight'.

13.20: Informed by Group that 49 and 83 Squadrons are to each bomb-up 6 aircraft to stand-by until further notice.

Obviously some operational capability was to be maintained, and this was confirmed on 25 December:

0945: Bomber Command stand-down, but aircraft on standby

were to remain as ordered.

14.25 Aircraft standing-by are to be prepared to operate at dawn tomorrow.

For Pilot Officer Robinson and his crew, normal services resumed on 28 December 1941 with a trip to Hüls (Op. 28) in the Rhine valley, where they dropped a land mine on a rubber factory. Then they took part in two missions to bomb battlecruisers at Brest (Ops. 29 and 30) on 5 and 10 January 1942, and Jack had survived his first operational tour. His chance of survival had been 44 per cent.[12] At that time the chance of surviving two tours was 19.5 per cent. The more he flew, the lower the chance of survival.

At this stage of the strategic bomber offensive, it could easily be argued that the harm inflicted could not justify the losses of both personnel and matériel. Fortunately, those who could see the benefits which new aircraft and navigation systems would bring to the battle were sufficiently determined to ensure that the fight continued to be taken to the enemy. As new radar and communications equipment were delivered to the bomber fleet, bombing accuracy improved enormously.

We will look later at the technological developments which Jack had to master during his career. However, it is worth looking now at Identification Friend or Foe (IFF), which is classed as a secondary radar system. Unlike a primary radar system, which sends out pulses of radio energy and then detects any echoes reflected back off large objects such as aircraft, a secondary radar causes a transponder on friendly vehicles to return a pulse with a secret code to the interrogating radar. IFF was deployed from 1939 to prevent friendly aircraft being attacked by RAF fighters. Once away from UK air defences, bomber crews were supposed to turn off their on-board IFF transponders in case the Germans learnt how to track them (which they did). Unfortunately, a rumour spread through Bomber Command to the effect that the IFF transponder signal somehow jammed the radars used by the Germans to direct searchlights. The rumour was false, but its resistance to being laid to rest is an indication of the difficulties of maintaining efficiency in a fast-moving technological environment. Overall, it is fair to claim that the RAF managed very well the introduction of new technologies during the Second World War, but the false IFF rumour was an example of the difficulties which could occur through ignorance.

Overall, the year 1941 had been a difficult year for Britain. Pushed onto the defensive at sea and on land, the air offensive was a constant reminder of intent, both to Germany and to friendly states. The bombing campaign also had overwhelming support from the British public. Whether the RAF on its own could ever have achieved the strategic air victory which was needed to assure the defeat of Germany is a matter of speculation. However, a crucial event occurred near to the end of the year when the Japanese navy attacked the USA at Pearl Harbor on 7 December 1941. President Roosevelt signed a declaration of war against Japan the next day. On that day Japanese bombers sunk HMS *Prince of Wales* and HMS *Repulse*, two battleships which were heading to north-east Malaya to intercept a Japanese convoy. Three days later Germany and Italy declared war on the USA, and on the same day Congress authorised the President to reciprocate. This was the pivotal moment which was to bring the might of the United States Army Air Force (USAAF) into the battle line.

Chapter 7

The Millennium Raids

The Hampden aircraft which Jack had flown in from Scampton had only two engines, ineffective heating and limited survivability. But the RAF was now bringing in new four-engine bombers more suited to long flights, with improved navigation systems and better survivability in battle. Their crews had to be trained to operate the new equipment, and those who had completed a tour of duty turned their hands to instruction duties. Leaving 49 Squadron on 8 February 1942, Jack went first to No. 16 Operational Training Unit at Upper Heyford, a few miles west of Bicester in Oxfordshire, where he became a member of the instructing staff. At the age of twenty-two he was an old hand.

Meanwhile, Air Chief Marshal Harris, now Commander-in-Chief Bomber Command, had been pondering his role. Put simply, his job was to put pressure on the German High Command, to divert resources to home defence, to disrupt the German munitions industry, and to show the German people that victory was not inevitable. He did not assume these responsibilities; they were given to him by the British War Cabinet. The difficulty facing Harris was that with the resources available he could not always concentrate his forces sufficiently well to have the strategic impact which he was required to achieve. On 28 March 1942, he had achieved the necessary concentration at Lübeck, but Lübeck was not a large well-defended city. To do the job he had been given, Harris had to achieve concentration of bombing in both space and time in major industrial cities. The Lübeck raid did have some impact. John Terraine records that Hitler's propagandist, Dr Goebbels wrote on 4 April 1942:

...it is horrible. One can well imagine how such an awful bombardment affects the population...we can't get away from the fact that the English [sic] air raids have increased in scope and importance; if they can be continued for weeks on these lines, they might conceivably have a demoralising effect on the population...

Goebbels was, in fact, wrong. The German people were highly resistant to being demoralised. Indeed, Terraine notes that the German population, with its natural powers of endurance stimulated by fear of the Gestapo, was tougher than either Goebbels or the British air staff imagined.[1]

From Harris's perspective, though, his command had to achieve wider destruction in a bigger target, preferably a large industrial city. He had one more test to try. The need for concentration was accepted as one of the prerequisites of a successful raid but another debate, not yet resolved, was what type of munitions to drop. The choice was between high explosives and incendiaries. Incendiaries had the bigger impact in congested areas, but factory and transport infrastructure seemed to require explosives. Harris decided on another trial of strength. Over four successive nights the town of Rostock was attacked. Despite clear nights and a full moon, the photographic evidence was initially disappointing. However, the third night showed some improvement, with severe damage to the Heinkel aircraft factory ; by the fourth night (26 April 1942) all photographs taken were within the target area. Goebbels wrote:

> The Führer is in extremely bad humour about the poor anti-aircraft defence...the *Luftwaffe* wasn't adequately prepared, and this alone made the damage of the Heinkel works possible.

In fact, the disruption did not last long. The authorities reported that the factories were back to full production within three days. Nevertheless, Harris had his evidence. The annihilation of an entire city was no longer a pipedream. Overwhelming concentration of force, and the correct ratio of high explosive and incendiary bombs, were able to destroy on a scale next to which a later generation's concept of 'shock and awe' would seem puny.

Even though a city may well be defended, the sheer numbers of the attacking aircraft would saturate the defences. Having reached this conclusion, Harris's next problem was to find the aircraft. He would need about 1,000 bombers. On an average day, Bomber Command had about 400 bombers serviceable and available for operations. Harris tried to borrow aircraft from Coastal Command and Flying Training Commands, to no avail, although Flying Training Command eventually lent four Wellingtons. Harris filled the gap by taking aircraft from the Operational Training Units, which were in his command. He detailed for the operation 598 Wellingtons, 131 Halifaxes, 88 Stirlings, 79 Hampdens, 73 Lancasters, 46 Manchesters, and 28 Whitleys, a total of 1,043 – virtually everything he had. The two Operational Training Groups provided 367 aircraft with crew drawn from both instructors and some pupils. The instructors were the most valuable asset being risked, as they were the aircrew who, like Jack, had operational experience. The operation was named Millennium. Two considerations influenced the timing of the raid: the need for clear air to reduce the risk of collisions over the target, and the need for a full moon to illuminate the city. The target was to be selected personally by Harris, as late as possible, on the basis of weather forecasts. Cologne drew the short straw.

Millennium was the biggest air raid ever. The 1,043 bombers were launched on 30 May 1942. Only 898 actually reached the target. One of them was Hampden P2138 from No. 16 Operational Training Unit, Upper Heyford, piloted by Flight Sergeant Riley, with Jack in the wireless operator's seat (Op. 31). They were airborne for 5 hours and 10 minutes. During the raid, 1,500 tons of bombs were dropped on the target in less than two hours. Germany's fourth largest city was set ablaze. Next day, air reconnaissance aircraft pilots could see from over the Dutch coast the pall of smoke, which reached up to 15,000 feet. The two spires of Cologne Cathedral remained intact, a fact claimed at the time as evidence of the accuracy of the bomb-aiming, although it was a fluke. Over forty aircraft failed to return, but a loss of less than 5 per cent of the number taking part was seen as acceptable, given the extent of damage achieved. Over 250 factories were destroyed or damaged, the enemy's manufacturing capability was severely hit, and disruption to the population reduced productivity in the munitions factories. Of the 1,500 tons of bombs dropped, about two-thirds were incendiaries. It was the fires started by the incendiary bombs which enabled all the bombers to find the target. Fire and explosives together did the damage, which was considerable. This single raid caused more damage in Cologne than all the previous seventy raids on the city put together. German authorities claimed that the city was functioning 'almost normally' within two weeks, but at what cost to the overall German war effort was not stated.

In his account of this operation, John Terraine[2] notes that there were not many occasions in the Second World War when Allied leaders were called upon to accept such risk and to decide matters of such moment. But Harris's decision brought belief, focus, and political support to the strategic bomber offensive. As the Official History of the RAF put it, Harris had proved himself as 'a Commander endowed with exceptional courage and resolution'.

The most remarkable factor of Millenium has not yet been mentioned. Almost beyond belief, it was repeated the following night. On 1 June 1942, 957 aircraft were detailed to attack Essen, reckoned to be a more demanding target than Cologne. Harris records rather laconically:[3]

> Since I had 1000 bombers mobilised and intact, I decided to send the whole force to Essen two nights later, and so continue the campaign against the Ruhr which I had been instructed to begin with such inadequate forces in the spring.

Jack flew with Flight Sergeant Riley again on the second Millenium raid (Op. 32), but they had to turn back when their starboard engine failed. This time, the weather forecasters failed to predict a sudden change which put 50 per cent cloud cover over the target. As a result, the Essen raid was not nearly as effective as at Cologne. Jack would have seen enough over Cologne to appreciate the potential of concentrated raids on cities. The trick was to ensure that the main force of bombers could identify the target and release their bombs in as short a time as possible. The enemy's ground defences were then overwhelmed. The theory of concentration, which Bomber Command staff had debated for over a year, was now accepted as the tactic best suited to the bombing strategy. To what degree the experience of the 1,000 bomber raids influenced Jack's increasing understanding of the principles of air warfare we cannot tell.

Jack remained at Upper Heyford until 12 August 1942. Apart from the two Millennium Raids he did very little flying, just five sorties in Hampdens and four in Wellingtons. Eventually, however, he was recalled to the fray with a posting to No. 14 Operational Training Unit (14 OTU) at RAF Cottesmore, in Rutland, where he stayed for four months. He was now a student again, being given air firing exercises, and taking the wireless operator's role in cross-country exercises. He flew mainly in Wellingtons, but also in Ansons and Hampdens. From October onwards, his pilot was Sergeant Hoover of the Royal Canadian Air Force (RCAF). They would fly together during two operational tours.

Harold Clifford Hoover was born in Yeomans, Saskatchewan, where he grew up. On 21 June 1941, nine days before Jack flew to Kiel and back on his first operation, Harold Hoover went to Regina, to enlist in the RCAF. Following basic military training at Edmonton, he learnt to fly at No. 6 Elementary Flying School at Prince Albert, graduating on 4 October 1941. He then went to No. 11 Service Flying Training School at Yorktown for his training in military flying, from which he graduated on 24 March 1942. Promoted to the rank of sergeant, he was posted on loan to RAF Bomber Command, more precisely to 14 OTU at RAF Cottesmore, where Sergeant Jack Mossop was converting to the Halifax. The informal process through which good crews assembled themselves then began. There is little evidence of the relationship between Jack and Harold Hoover. Saskatchewan is a very big area, and very under-populated, at least when compared with Great Britain. There is a suggestion that Hoover was a loner by nature, and not particularly concerned about the niceties of life. On the other hand, there is ample evidence that he was a superb pilot, which for a bomber crew is the attribute most desired. His crew did not use his first names; he was always referred to as Hoover or 'Hoov'.

Altogether Jack logged 44 hours and 40 minutes in the air while at Cottesmore. His end-of-course summary of flying and assessments, Form 414(A), pasted into his flying log is again signed by a wing commander with an illegible signature. It does record, however, that Jack's ability in both signals and air gunnery was still above average. Jack Mossop, Harold Hoover, and, as it turned out, the future members of a new crew, were posted to No. 102 Conversion Unit at RAF Pocklington, twelve miles to the east of the City of York, to be trained on the four-engined Halifax bomber. The standard time required to convert a crew to a heavy (i.e. four-engined) bomber was forty flying hours. Jack had a total of fifteen hours in daylight and two hours in night flying, spread over eight flights and eight weeks, during which he was allowed three weeks' leave during Christmas and New Year.

In January 1943, while Jack was still on leave, Winston Churchill met President Roosevelt in Casablanca. One of their conclusions was that the UK and the USA should join forces in a strategic air assault on Germany. It was agreed that the United States Army Air Force (USAAF) would establish bases in England from which they would attack Germany by day, whilst Bomber Command would maintain its campaign at night, creating round-the-clock bombing of Germany. Air Marshal Harris at Bomber Command was told:[4]

> Your primary object will be the progressive destruction and dislocation of the German military, industrial and economic system, and the undermining of the morale of the German people to a point where their capacity for armed resistance is fatally weakened.

The directive also allowed for other targets of a more tactical nature, such the ships of the German Navy wherever they could be found and, importantly given the continuing threat to Allied ships in the Atlantic, submarine bases on the coast of Biscay. A later addition to the directive was that Berlin should be attacked as often as possible. This was to encourage Russia to press forward following the surrender of the German 6th Army at Stalingrad.

Chapter 8

The Second Tour

Jack was posted to 76 Squadron on 30 January 1943, along with the other six members of the new crew. The squadron was stationed at RAF Linton-on-Ouse, where it was about to have its motto *Resolute* severely tested. Having made his point with the 1,000 bomber raids, Air Marshal Harris was about to launch what became known as the Battle of the Ruhr. A large proportion of Germany's industrial capability was located in the part of the valley where the Ruhr flows into the Rhine. Cities such as Essen, Duisberg, and Dortmund were attacked several times during the period 5 March to 12 July 1943. In fact, the battle was not constrained to the Ruhr valley. Berlin, Stuttgart, and Munich were also targeted several times during this phase of the bombing campaign. The aim was entirely strategic: to reduce the ability of the enemy to wage war by destroying as much as possible of his munitions manufacturing capability. Oil refineries and depots were a particular type of high priority target.

Much had changed since Jack's first tour had been completed a year previously. New four-engined aircraft, Stirlings and Halifaxes were being delivered, with Lancasters yet to come, and the scientific boffins at the Telecommunications Research Establishment (TRE) had devised ways of using radio signals to guide bombers to their targets.

It was not only the aircraft which the new crews had to get used to; tactics had also changed. The Pathfinder Force (PFF) had been formed in August 1942. Crews had been selected and trained to apply tactical control over the bombers' targets. They dropped flares to mark the aiming points to be used by the bomb-aimers of the main force of bombers. The concept of a Master Bomber had also evolved. An experienced crew would provide a running commentary by radio, controlling the bombing by reference to flares and visible ground features.

The crew Jack had trained with when converting to the Halifax had been posted together to 76 Squadron. The value of keeping crews together as much as possible had been learnt. Confidence in the competence of other crew members, and even knowledge of minor flaws, led to trust within the team, and greater effectiveness. Unlike 49 Squadron in 1941, 76 Squadron in 1943 maintained a thorough record of operations in their F540 ORB. From this we can ascertain the surnames of Hoover's crew; for providing their first names I must thank Bill Lloyd, the flight engineer:

Sergeant Harold Clifford Hoover RCAF (pilot)

Sergeant Geof Howden RCAF (navigator)

Sergeant Kenneth Bergey RCAF (bomb-aimer)

Sergeant Jack Mossop RAF (wireless operator)

Sergeant Gordon William (Bill) Lloyd, RAF (flight engineer)

Sergeant Clifford Alan Hill RAF (mid-upper gunner)

Flight Sergeant Patrick Tripp RCAF (rear gunner)

Max Hastings points out that No. 76 was an exceptionally international squadron with a strong contingent of Norwegians as well as other nationalities.[1] Canadians were also numerous. There were four in Jack's crew, including the pilot. Cliff Hill, the mid-upper gunner, described Hoover as a tough Canadian from Saskatchewan who would introduce himself, 'Ahm from Regina'. He was powerfully built with dark hair, and he had a quirky sense of humour. Hoover was the youngest of all his crew and when he was posted in he was the youngest pilot in 76 Squadron. He was only nineteen years old when he flew his first operation in February 1943. The oldest in Hoover's crew was 'Howdy' Howden, who was thirty-two. Jack Mossop was twenty-three when he joined the squadron.

Apart from Jack they were all on their first tour. There can be no doubt that Jack's previous experience was to be of great value to the new crew, but it seems that his first intervention was to say to Gordon Lloyd, 'Who ever heard of an engineer called Gordon? Haven't you got another name?'. William, Lloyd's second name nearly sufficed, but Jack decided that Bill would be best. And Gordon Lloyd was thereafter called Bill through a long flying career extending through two tours in Bomber Command and a successful career in civilian flying after the war ended. Only in recent years have the majority of his acquaintances known him as Gordon. By all accounts available in family folk-lore, this re-naming of a colleague was typical of Jack Mossop. It seems that he carried a natural authority which his colleagues respected and accepted. Or maybe he was just cheeky.

The commanding officer of 76 Squadron when Jack reported for duty was one of the RAF's greatest pilots, Wing Commander Leonard Cheshire. The son of a distinguished lawyer, Cheshire had himself read law at Cambridge. He had joined the RAF before the war began, and he built up his reputation through meticulous attention to detail, both in his dealings with subordinates and in his approach to flying. In his book *Bomber Command*,[2] Max Hastings notes that unlike some squadron commanders, Cheshire always chose the most dangerous raids when he flew on operations. Excepting only a wireless operator, Jock Hill, Cheshire did not have his own crew; when he went on a raid he flew 'second dickey', alongside the regular pilot, who would usually be the newest and most nervous on the squadron. However, he did not fly with Hoover's crew, although Jock Hill twice stood in as wireless operator, on 27 and 29 March, when Jack had a bout of flu.

Nine miles north-west of York, the airfield at Linton-on-Ouse was built under the 1936/38 expansion scheme. The camp of brick, flat-roofed permanent buildings was immediately adjacent to the village of Linton-on-Ouse and at the south-east corner of the landing ground. Its five Type C hangars provided good facilities for the squadrons, of which the first to arrive were Nos. 51 and 58, both flying Whitleys.

When built, Linton was the premier airfield in No. 4 Group,

which also had its headquarters on the base. However, the landing strips were prone to water-logging in winter, despite attempts to drain the airfield. It thus became only the second Bomber Command airfield to have concrete runways. The two runways were initially both just over 1,100 yards long and were completed in August 1939. Whitley aircraft were dispatched from Linton-on-Ouse on operations on the first night of the war, dropping propaganda leaflets over northern Europe. During the summer of 1942 the two runways were extended to 2,000 yards and just under 1,500 yards, and a third runway of 1,400 yards was built. A concrete perimeter track was also provided, giving access to the runways from thirty-four aircraft hard standings. The resident squadrons were regularly detached to other bases while the runways were built. The building activity at Linton-on-Ouse must have attracted the attention of the *Luftwaffe*, because on the night of 10 May 1941 at least three enemy aircraft bombed the base. The Station Commander, Group Captain Frederick Garraway, was one of several people killed.

Early in 1941, Linton had received the first deliveries of the brand new Halifax four-engined bombers. No. 35 Squadron, in which Jack was to serve during his third tour in 1944, was re-formed to undertake service acceptance trials, and in due course a second Halifax squadron was formed, in May 1941, by taking C Flight from 35 Squadron and re-designating it as No. 76 Squadron. 35 Squadron remained at Linton-on-Ouse until August 1942 when, having been selected to become a Pathfinder unit, it was transferred to No. 8 Group and the new airfield at Graveley. 76 Squadron stayed at Linton until the base was transferred to the RCAF.

At the time when Hoover and his crew were posted to 76 Squadron early in 1943 there was a shortage of accommodation at Linton-on-Ouse. The RAF had purloined part of Beningbrough Hall as overflow dormitory space. The hall, built in 1716, is about eight miles north of York. In 1943 it belonged to Lady Chesterfield, but it is now in the hands of The National Trust, whose handbook for 2006 notes its cantilevered stairs, exceptional wood carving, and an unusual central corridor.[3] This was a big improvement over the accommodation at Pocklington which had been definitely below par. Cliff Hill

56

recalled their life at Beningbrough in a monograph written at the time when Kevin Wilson was collecting material for his book *Bomber Boys*. I am grateful to Bill Lloyd for sending me a copy of Cliff's text.

They arrived on a cold day in late January 1943. As they unloaded their kit from the truck they were somewhat amazed at their new accommodation. According to Cliff Hill's account, Pat Tripp said, 'Gee, a piece of old England'; Bill Lloyd said 'only the best'; and Hoover, who liked his food, said 'any chow?' Jack Mossop simply said, correctly, 'Georgian' – no doubt it was the benefits of his family's self-teaching regime coming through. Hoover's crew were allocated two rooms on the top floor of the house. The Canadians took one, and Jack, Bill Lloyd, and Cliff Hill were in the other, along with three NCOs from other crews. The occupants of the three extra beds changed frequently as the risk equation caught up with them, and they failed to return from operations. One group lasted only three nights before their personal effects were removed. This was a little disheartening, to the point that it was agreed that the crew could have sole use of the two rooms. If they were shot down they would all go together. Having half-crews disappearing before they could get to know them was not good for morale. Cliff Hill noted the contrast between the peace and tranquillity of Beningbrough and the hell at the sharp end of their work. Early 1943 was a period of heavy losses in Bomber Command, and the expectation of completing a full tour seemed very low. Cliff for one believed that he would never survive the tour.

Their daily routine involved cycling two and a half miles to Linton in the morning and returning in the evening or, if they were detailed for an operation, early the next morning. They had the use of the main entrance and hall, and a room on the first floor where there was a grand piano for which there was usually a competent pianist in residence, and where for a while they even had a bar. Lady Chesterfield was not in residence; she had moved out to the Home Farm on the estate. Her furniture was stored safely in locked rooms. Cliff Hill's words have found their way into the National Trust guide to the house: for the aircrew billeted there, it was an oasis of peace in a world turned inside out by the nature of their duties. Only the composition of the crew had any continuity, and even that could be short-lived – Cliff Hill's gun turret perspex was spattered by naval guns over the Friesians on their second operation of the tour; no one was hurt, but sooner or later the wheel of fortune would turn. There were many women serving in the WAAF on the base, but long-term relationships were almost impossible to manage, especially in a society which still expected marriage before sex.

Three types of four-engined bombers were used by the RAF in the Second World War. The Short Stirling was the first into service in August 1940, but by 1943 it was withdrawn from the strategic bomber offensive as too vulnerable. The type next into service, the Handley Page Halifax, was in the front line for longer, indeed until the end of the war. The first Halifax was delivered to 35 Squadron at RAF Leeming in November 1940. The squadron moved to Linton-on-Ouse on 5 December 1940, where it suffered many teething troubles with its new aircraft. They did not fly operationally until 10 March 1941, when the squadron attacked Le Havre. The third four-engined type was, of course, the Lancaster, which we will come to in a later chapter.

Despite set-backs during its acceptance into service, the Halifax eventually became a reliable war-horse. With four Rolls-Royce Merlin engines, it could achieve 265 mph, and it had an operational range of 1,860 miles carrying 5,800 lb of bombs. The major shortcoming of the Halifax was its operational ceiling, which at 17,500 ft was not high enough to be safe from flak. It had a crew of seven: pilot, flight engineer, navigator, bomb-aimer, rear gunner, mid-upper gunner and wireless operator. A total of 6,176 Halifaxes were delivered to the RAF, the last delivery being in November 1946. Later marks of Halifax were used as parachute troop carriers and as glider tugs. It was the only RAF aircraft cleared to tow the Horsa troop glider; the first operation in this role was on 19 November 1942 when two Horsa gliders were towed to southern Norway for the attack on a German heavy water plant. The last Halifax in RAF service made its final sortie on 17 March 1952.

The Mark I Halifax had two beam gun turrets but in the Mark II bomber version, operated by 76 Squadron in 1943, the beam turrets were replaced by a dorsal mounted gun turret. A rear gunner and a mid-upper gunner were thus detailed in the crew composition. The bomb-aimer's position was at the front of the aircraft, below the front gun turret, about fifteen feet forward of the pilot. The navigator was below and forward of the pilot's cockpit, and the flight engineer was behind the pilot. The wireless operator's cubicle was below the pilot's cockpit. When first brought into service, the Halifax had a front turret mounted above the bomb-aimer's station but this was removed after it was found that it was rarely used.

The wireless operator in a Halifax had much more sophisticated set of equipment than Jack had used in the Hampdens during 1941. Halifax aircraft had a new radio transmitter, the Type 1154, and a new receiver Type R1155. These two types of radio were still in service when I joined the RAF in 1962, and possibly also when I left the RAF in 1996. Other equipment in the Halifax wireless operator's den was much as described in Chapter 6, but the layout of the desk and the accessibility of controls were much improved over the Hampden installation. There were also two significant additions. A control unit for Identification Friend or Foe (IFF) installation was mounted on the left hand side of the work table. Let us assume that Jack would have not been taken in by the rumours that the IFF frequency could blind the German's radar controlled anti-aircraft guns. Jack would be responsible for setting the correct code on the IFF unit so that the UK air defence radar system could identify his aircraft as friendly when interrogated. He would also have to switch the IFF responder off as soon as they flew out of the airspace controlled by Fighter Command, remembering to switch it back on again when they were on the way home. The second improvement was the presence at Jack's work-station of two hot air ducts. One of the possible consequences of flying in Bomber Command, frost-bite, had been removed. There were other benefits of flying in what was a much larger aeroplane that the Hampden. Jack's parachute, for instance, was stowed immediately behind his seat. There was even a stowage box for a spare trailing aerial which could be deployed if the first one should be come detached or broken.

Hoover's crew flew their first operation in their new squadron on 16 February 1943. They had arrived at a critical moment in the bombing campaign. Four engines were now more common than two in the Bomber Command order of battle, and the Pathfinders had new electronic navigation and bombing aids to identify the targets. If Bomber Command could not now reliably hit targets at the heart of German industry, its campaign would fail. We will return in the next chapter to the crucial advantage which technological developments would bring to the bombing campaign

As it happened, Hoover's crew headed away from Germany to find their first target of the tour. On 16 February 1943 they flew to Lorient (Op. 33) which Jack had previously visited on 23 November 1941. This time, we have a record of their report to the intelligence officer who would have debriefed the crew, and which the squadron adjutant (or his clerk) had written into the 76 Squadron ORB:

> Target visually identified also by PFF flares. Target in bombsight but bombs not seen to explode. Numerous fires and one large explosion seen in target area. No opposition. encountered. Photograph shows faint ground detail. Good effort for the navigator who was on his first trip.

'PFF flares' refers to the markers dropped by the Pathfinder Force – the first time Jack would have seen them, certainly in operational flying. Geoff Howden was not the only member of the crew who was on his first trip, but navigation was so critical to success that the crew would be relieved that their rookie navigator had passed his first test. The navigator was not on his own able to guarantee navigational accuracy. The planning of each raid included the route to be taken, and the choice of route was heavily dependent on the meteorological forecasts, particularly wind strength and direction. The forecast could be updated by radio messages once the aircraft were airborne, but a major error in the initial forecast could have a significant impact on the accuracy of navigation.

All RAF bombers had been fitted with automatic flash cameras since Jack had left the fray. They gave the only credible evidence of the accuracy of the bombing. Jack frequently commented on the quality of the photographs he brought back. The photographs were handed out to the bomber crews and formed the basis of the squadron 'bombing ladder'.[4] The overall score of each squadron was sent to Group headquarters and then on to Bomber Command.

Some things had not changed. The approaches to the north German naval bases were still being mined, and on 18 February 1943 they were detailed for a gardening operation, laying mines off Langeoog (Op. 34), which is in the middle of the string of the Frisian Islands north of Wilhelmshaven. The Squadron ORB records that four aircraft took part and that all returned, one with minor damage. That was Hoover's aircraft BB282, tail letter P Peter, hit by shrapnel from naval ships on only the second time they had flown it to war. The aircraft fuselage was holed, but no one was hurt. BB282 was named Pinocchio by the ground crew, according to Cliff Hill, because Hoover had a prominent nose. A suitably garish rendition of Pinocchio was duly painted on the aircraft's nose while the aircraft was in a hangar for repairs.

The repairs did not take long. The following day they attacked Wilhelmshaven (Op. 35) The ORB records:

Identified target by PFF. Flares and ground markers in bombsight when bombs were released at 2326 from 13,000 ft. Incendiaries seen to explode and fires taking hold. Flares placed in position 15 mins too late. No opposition encountered. Photo shows slight ground detail. Good navigation.

Because it was crucial to the success of a raid, the quality of navigation was a factor on which the debriefing intelligence officer would always inquire. The responses are not always recorded in the squadron ORB.

Then there was a five-day gap, before they were off to Nuremburg (Op. 36). For some reason neither of the ORBs makes any mention of this raid. However, there is a record from another source. Jack later told his wife that he once met the renowned Wing Commander Guy Gibson, by chance, in a pub somewhere near a bomber base. Like many of his colleagues, he recognised in Gibson the mettle of a true warrior. During his tour with 76 Squadron, Jack twice flew on the same raids as Gibson, who was then only a few months away from becoming a national hero through his leadership of 617 Squadron and the Dambuster raid. At this time Gibson was the Commanding Officer of 106 Squadron, based at RAF Syerston near Newark-on-Trent. The entry in 106 Squadron's ORB for 25 February 1943 raid on Nuremburg reads:[5]

> Conditions very good for bombing: no cloud, excellent visibility. Target located visually and bombed from 12,000ft. A very concentrated attack which caused fires and explosions. A good but frightening trip – aircraft circling round waiting for the PFF. Rather dangerous.

The Pathfinders were supposed to be there first. Either the planning was faulty, or the PFF was late. The most significant variable which could upset the plan and cause late or early arrival was the wind. As noted above, the bombers followed set routes to the target designed both to avoid enemy defences and to disguise their target, but if they encountered wind conditions different from the forecast the plan could easily be upset. On the next day, 26 February, 76 Squadron and 106 Squadron were both tasked to attack Cologne (Op. 37). Gibson was more impressed this time, writing in his flying log:

> Operations: Cologne. A wizard prang. Huge fires. Moderate flak. Same load. My 169th war flight.

Gibson had such a large number of operations in his log book because after a first tour flying Hampdens he had served a tour with Fighter Command, flying Bristol Beaufighters with 29 Squadron at RAF Digby. The Beaufighter was a very effective night-fighter fitted with a forward looking air interception radar system able to detect attacking German bombers. The 106 Squadron ORB record of the Cologne raid on 25 February was more prosaic than Gibson's own account:

> Weather good, slight ground haze but river and ground detail seen, these were in sights, bombing in a straight, fast (220 IAS) run from 16,000 ft at 2121 hours. Bombs seen to burst near aiming point. Concentration was achieved and it seemed that the target had been accurately bombed. Heavy flak encountered in barrage form. This was pilot's 70th bombing raid.

In contrast, the entry in the 76 Squadron ORB for the Cologne raid on 26 February 1943 reads rather sparsely:

> 17 ac detailed but only 15 attacked target; one did not take off because of a coolant leak.

Gibson had only one more operation with 106 Squadron, on 11 March. Within two and a half months he had then formed a new squadron, number 617, trained its crews in very low-level bombing tactics with a new type of bomb, and breached the Möhne and Eder dams. The famous Dambuster raid took place on 16 May 1943, a classic example of strategic target selection.

Despite the lack of follow-up attacks, the dams raid was a spectacular success, and it also showed the value of a tactical commander over the target area. Having delivered his mine onto the Möhne dam, Gibson stayed in the target area and gave orders to his squadron as they, one by one, made their hazardous run in to the weapon release point. When the Möhne dam collapsed Gibson then led his surviving aircraft to the Eder. The concept of an airborne tactical commander in the target area had been developed and tested overnight.[6]

The lessons were sometimes learnt the hard way; sometimes it seemed simple. St Nazaire (Op. 38) was the next target for Hoover and his crew, on 28 February 1943. The squadron ORB records:

> 15 ac detailed for raid; 14 took off, all returned safely. Railway main target. Target visually identified and attacked at 2432 from 16,000 ft. Several small fires over the whole area of the town. No opposition encountered.

After that it was Berlin (Op. 39), on 1 March 1943:

> All of the Squadron's best crews were in on this attack. It is reckoned that the German capital suffered its worst blow of the present war. PFF very accurate with their marker flares and consequently the HE rained down upon the concentration, creating the worst damage Berlin has ever experienced. It is deeply regretted that the Squadron lost two of its finest crews, including two captains (Squadron Leader Fletcher and

Flying Officer Black) who had been an inspiration to the Squadron as well as to their crews.

76 Squadron contributed fourteen Halifax aircraft to this raid. Hoover's crew returned unharmed and with no damage, but their flight commander, Squadron Leader James Fletcher was lost. Someone on the squadron, probably Leonard Cheshire, decided that this raid was sufficiently different to justify a fulsome summary in the ORB:

> This was a very important target for the first attack of the month, and a very successful job was made of it. 14 of our aircraft were briefed for this raid, and the cream of the squadron was chosen. A very large force from Bomber Command arrived over the target at the appointed time, and as the Pathfinders had been very precise with their marker flares the damage done by HE and incendiaries dropped around the concentration of marker flares, the damage done was most devastating. Fires could be seen concentrated over the entire target area and the glow was observed as far as Hanover when the ac were returning. It is deeply regretted that the Squadron lost two of its best crews in the raid. Both Squadron Leader Fletcher and Flying Officer Black had been an inspiration to their flight and the loss will be felt for some time to come. One other ac landed at Swanton Morely.

After this raid, Jack remarked to his crew-mates:

> Now that you have been to the 'Big City' you might just survive, as long as I am with you.

Cliff Hill later wrote that he had great faith in Jack and believed everything he said; Jack was the only man he met who showed no fear in any way.

The next night they were stood down and they made their way to 'The Briefing Room', otherwise known as Betty's Bar, in York. This famous establishment, which is now an equally famous tea-house, was a magnet for aircrew in the many squadrons based in Yorkshire, hence its RAF nickname. Apart from the occasional mess dance there was little entertainment on the station. In any case, the increasing pace of operations would allow little time for entertainment. Including the Berlin raid described above, Hoover and his crew flew in six raids in the thirteen days from 1 to 12 March 1943, attacking Berlin, Hamburg (Op. 40), Essen (Op. 41), Nuremberg (Op. 42), Munich (Op. 43) and Essen (Op. 44) again. The Berlin, Nuremburg and Munich raids each required over eight hours in the air. The two raids on Essen on 5 and 12 March were of particular importance as they demolished much of the Krupps armament factories in the city. Harris deemed the first of the two Essen raids as the best since he had taken charge of Bomber Command. The Pathfinders used the new radio navigation system, Oboe, to find the target, and of the 392 aircraft which bombed, only fourteen (3.6 per cent) were lost.[7] The Ruhr Valley or 'Happy Valley' as it was known to all in Bomber Command, was fast becoming very familiar to Jack and his crewmates.

Any sense of familiarity had to be seen in context. Each operation carried a significant risk of not returning. The principle risk, of course, was death, with serious injury not far behind. Risk of capture should it be necessary to bale out and parachute onto enemy territory carried a lesser consequence, provided the first person encountered did not shoot you. The aircraft interior was itself hazardous, both to the safety of the crew and to their health, but the aircrew were mostly fit young men, and the health risk was mainly psychiatric. For those whose nerves were frayed there was little way out. Lack of moral fibre was the usual official conclusion, leading to stripping of rank, and an ignoble conclusion to a career which in kinder times would have been saved through appropriate treatment.

The entry from 76 Squadron's ORB for 3 March 1943 reads:

The Pathfinders had once again done a grand job and the marksmanship of the Air Bombers was first class. The glow from fires could be seen 100 miles away. One ac, Flying Officer Golding, failed to return.

The target had been Hamburg (Op. 40). Two days later the Battle of the Ruhr officially began. Jack would later seem almost nostalgic about the Ruhr, but in fact only twelve of his ninety operations were against targets in the Ruhr Valley. However, his next operation marked the start of the battle; Essen was the target, on 5 March (Op. 41). Essen was a difficult target. Deep in the Ruhr Valley, it had a permanent industrial haze; it was as well protected as Berlin by searchlights and anti-aircraft guns; and it was surrounded by other large towns including Dortmund, Duisberg, and Düsseldorf which created problems in target identification.

This raid is described in some detail by Max Hastings in his book *Bomber Command*.[8] It was led by Pathfinder Mosquitoes equipped with the Oboe blind navigation system, which enabled accurate placing of the target indicators. 76 Squadron Halifaxes were in the first wave of the main force which comprised 443 aircraft and included Wellingtons, Stirlings and Lancasters. Only fourteen aircraft (3.2 per cent) were lost. Two-thirds of the bombs dropped were incendiaries; for it had now been determined that fire was more destructive than blast. High explosive bombs were still used but mainly to create channels along which the fires could flow. 76 Squadron's ORB for 5 March 1943 records:

> The target was the largest armament factory in the world – Krupps. (Hoover's crew) saw their bombs land close to markers; one terrific explosion at 2109. There was one loss: Flight Sergeant Milan's crew.

The Krupps factory was attacked by Bomber Command with almost obsessional zeal, as perhaps it should have been, given that it was a target well within the War Cabinet's instructions for attacking strategic targets. Overall, this raid was deemed highly successful. One hundred and fifty-three aircraft (out of 443) had dropped their weapons within three miles of the aiming point.[9] That only 35 per cent of the attacking force could hit a target six miles across was still unsatisfactory, but it was nonetheless an improvement on the estimate of 22 per cent calculated by Mr Butt in 1941, and the heavier bomb load carried by the new aircraft had a big impact on the effectiveness of each hit. Indeed, 160 acres of Essen had been flattened.

Three days later on the dark, cloudy night of 8 March, the

target was Nuremberg (Op. 42). This raid was something of a watershed for Jack Mossop. On the outward leg of the sortie, his rank was flight sergeant. On the return leg, after midnight, he was a pilot officer. His Form 453, airman's record of service, records that acting Flight Sergeant Mossop was discharged on 8 March 1943 under King's Regulation 652(14). The cause of this discharge was 'On appointment to a temporary commission'. The following day, a clerk in a different branch of the RAF Records Office raised a Form 1406 to record Jack's career as a commissioned officer. He had a new service number, 144165, but he remained in the RAF Volunteer Reserve 'for the duration of the emergency'. The practical implications of this promotion would initially have been mundane. He would be paid more, although not by much, and he would have moved into the Officers' Mess, where his mess bills would cost him more than they would in the Sergeants' Mess. However, Cheshire was a strong believer that all air crew should mix socially. Their off-base lodging at Beningbrough was ideal for a crew with a mix of commissioned and non-commissioned ranks. His status in the crew would be little changed. They had flown together often enough to know the strengths and weaknesses of each other. Officers were (and still are) expected to show leadership qualities at a higher level than that expected of non-commissioned ranks, and it is reasonable to assume that reports raised by Jack's squadron commanders, on both 49 and 76 Squadrons, had identified a level of leadership ability appropriate to commissioned service.

The night job was unchanged, however. The following day, 9 March, it was Munich (Op. 43). The ORB entry for the Munich raid illustrates the concerns which still existed over the effectiveness of the bombing:

All 11 ac returned safely – a good effort but 'not one of our best'. Markers were scattered.

'Not one of our best' is a phrase typical of Jack, as we shall see when this story reaches 1944. For now there was a short period without operations, and Hoover's crew went to a mess dance, probably in the Sergeants' Mess. They always socialised as a crew. There would have been 200 or so members of the WAAF on the base, and a dance was one of the few recreational activities available. Jack did not dance, but he would have enjoyed a few beers.

Hoover's crew flew next to Essen (Op. 44), on 12 March 1943. The squadron ORB entry is brief, but it succinctly details the two hazards of the bombing effort. Mechanical difficulties were as much a hazard as enemy action:

> 11 crews detailed to attack Essen – only 8 got there. Wing Commander Smith had to jettison bombs and crashed on landing – the ac was written off but none of the crew was injured. Flight Sergeant Clarke had to return to base because the undercarriage would not retract; he landed successfully. Flight Sergeant Nevine's crew were lost over the target.

Then the weather closed in and for two weeks the squadron was grounded. They thought that they might get some leave, but the squadron had been given two weeks leave early in February. They spent the time on aircraft evacuation and dinghy drills, aircraft recognition lessons, and attending lectures on subjects such as aircraft recognition and escape and evasion should they have to parachute into enemy territory. Cheshire even took them on a march through the Yorkshire countryside, with cheering as they re-entered the camp to show that their morale was good.

There was time then for further recreation. The seven men known as Hoover's crew toured York, visiting the Minster, walking along the river, going to the cinema, and always finishing off at Betty's. After they had seen all the sights of York they turned their attention to a pub which was only a mile from Beningbrough Hall, but unfortunately on the wrong side of the River Ouse. In winter regular visits were not feasible, but as spring brought lighter evenings and warmer weather, there was a ferry service, of sorts, across the river which took passengers to the village of Nun Monkton, and it was then only a short walk to the Alice Hawthorn pub.

The Alice Hawthorn was integral to the off-duty activities of airmen at Linton. When last visited in 2006, the notice board in the pub still displayed a short essay on the establishment by an anonymous member of 76 Squadron:

After our evening meal we were off exploring the grounds of Beningbrough Hall making our way over the lush green meadows in front of the house and down to where the River Ouse flowed through the estate. It was a still quiet evening and how wonderful to be alive and to gaze on this beautiful part of Yorkshire.

Along the river bank we came upon a gentleman known as Nick who owned a rowing boat and was doing a roaring trade ferrying RAF boys across the river so that they could visit the Alice Hawthorn pub in the beautiful village of Nun Monkton, so we paid our few pennies and were soon climbing up the opposite bank on our way to explore this new drinking place.

What a beautiful village this turned out to be. In front of the pub was a village green with a maypole and a duck pond at one end. I was intrigued with the various types of houses that surrounded the green as many of them seemed pretty old, although some were of brick construction, they all seemed in a pretty good state of repair and had been well looked after. The whole scene looking from the pub window was one of peace and tranquillity, and a far cry from what we had experienced over the Ruhr Valley on the previous night. The Alice Hawthorn proved to be a friendly pub and where happy chatter and a bit of community singing seemed to be the order of the day.

A newspaper cutting on the same pub notice board reads:

The crews at Beningbrough made good use of the ferrymen who took them across the River Ouse to enjoy a few beers at the Alice Hawthorn pub in Nun Monkton. These ferrymen certainly had an eye to business. They would charge twopence to cross the river – anything up to half a crown for the return journey after 9pm.

'The alternative was an 11-mile walk via Aldwark Bridge', said Bill Steel, a retired RAF sergeant. Bill was curator of the Memorial Room at Linton, dedicated to all ranks who served at the base during the war, until his death in 1982.

This fits in with Cliff Hill's description:

The ferryman was known as 'Captain Nick'. On seeing potential customers on the far side of the river, he would fetch his oars and row across. The charge was 2d per person one way, and 6d to take the passenger back. The last boat was at 10.30pm. As they were often late coming back from the Alice Hawthorn, they all looked at Hoover to produce a sizable tip to entice Captain Nick into his boat. Canadians were paid more than their RAF colleagues.

The anonymous author from 76 Squadron quoted above was quite correct in noting the beauty of the village, which by road can only be approached down a four mile dead-end. The village dates back to Norman times and lies on the River Ouse at the point where the River Nidd joins the Ouse. It is a very attractive village with an inspiring church and many fine buildings. Cattle and other animals roam at will around the central meadow, and duck and geese inhabit the pond.

There can be no doubt that the welcome the airmen received at the Alice Hawthorn was of immense value to morale at Linton, a value which would be enhanced many times when the North Yorkshire airfields of the RAF were given over to the RCAF. The inhabitants of Nun Monkton also deserve praise for their forbearance of what was soon to engulf them.

On 26 March Hoover's crew were back in Pinocchio, the aircraft they had used since late February, en route to Duisberg (Op. 45). The ORB had little to say:

10/10 cloud. Flares not visible, bombed on ETA

10/10 cloud means no sight of the ground. Bombing on estimated time of arrival (ETA) is a pathetic action in terms of expecting any harm to the enemy, but it does marginally increase the prospect of a safe return. An aircraft laden with bombs is restricted in manoeuvrability, and in range.

As already noted, Jack missed the next trip, which was to Berlin on 29 March, because he had flu. His place was taken by Cheshire's wireless operator, Jock Hill. It was a terrible night with severe icing on aircraft and low cloud, which hampered the navigators and obscured the target. 76 Squadron lost two crews, those of Flight Lieutenant Wetherley and Sergeant Curesly, and the final result was that out of 481 aircraft dispatched, six turned back and only three (less than 1 per cent) bombed within three miles of the aiming point.[10]   This was the only time Hoover turned back before reaching the target.   His aircraft was becoming uncontrollable because of icing, but he refused to jettison his bombs, probably to the consternation of his crew. They need not have worried. Despite having the extra weight of the bombs on board Hoover made his customary perfect three-point landing at Linton. As Bill Lloyd remembers, it was a firm but well-controlled landing.

Events were better managed on 3 April 1943, when Hoover and his crew were detailed for another raid on the Krupps munitions factory at Essen (Op. 46).   The compiler of the ORB seems content to congratulate the defences at Essen – easy enough when casualties are restricted to one crew and the attack has for once been provably successful:

A devastating attack on the centre of the Krupps works in Essen – the East and West wings of this famous works had been subjected to terrific bombing. And it was now the duty of the crews detailed to put the remaining part of the works out of action.

Photos showed that the centre was completely 'plastered'. One ac failed to return.

Defences over this target had been improved and both heavy and light flak were working in fine cooperation with the many searchlights.

All very well, but the difference between one lost aircraft and two is a very fine line. Cliff Hill, the mid-upper gunner in this tour, later wrote down his memories of 3/4 April 1943.   As they approached the target they watched a Lancaster slowly succumb to a German fighter and fall to the ground, and they saw ahead of them a terrific barrage of flak and hundreds of searchlight beams. The bomb-aimer, Ken Bergey, prone in the nose, called for the bomb doors to be opened. As they started their run-in they were caught by a radar controlled searchlight.   Immediately twenty or more other searchlights coned their Halifax. Ken, blinded by the searchlights, could not see any target markers, and the aircraft was being hit by shrapnel. Cliff was expecting Hoover to jettison the bombs and get out of the target area. Instead, Hoover swore and said that when they got out they would have to go round again. Using all his great strength, he twisted and turned the Halifax in the bright light. Nobody spoke as he wrestled with the controls, but they knew that they were silhouetted against a dark background above them. Above the roar of the engines the crump of exploding shells could be heard. Then Jack Mossop's voice was heard on the intercom, speaking calmly from his seat below the cockpit:

> Try putting her into a shallow dive, give her all you have got, and head for open country.

As recalled by Cliff, Hoover's reply was 'Roger Dodger, anything to get out of this mess'. It worked. The anti-aircraft gunners lost them as quickly as they had found them. A quick check to find out no one was injured and Hoover turned for another run. They had to cross the incoming bomber stream at an angle in order to get back on to the correct heading for another bombing run. Two collisions were narrowly avoided, and when they were back on track for another bombing run, the navigator mockingly criticised the pilot for being fifteen minutes late.

So they started again, running in at 19,000 ft at 2215 hours. Ken Bergey called bomb doors open as flak again burst around them. As he said 'bombs gone' they were hit again. Bill Lloyd announced that the starboard outer engine no longer worked. Still, Hoover held the aircraft straight and level, waiting for the flash which told him that the automatic photograph had been taken – he wanted the evidence that that they had bombed the target. But then they were again coned by searchlights. Flack hit the fuselage with a smell of cordite. Hoover twisted the aircraft through the air on three engines and then again dived to shake off the searchlights. They flew home on three engines, and Hoover made his usual perfect touch down at Linton. They landed at fifteen minutes past midnight, to find that the briefing room was full of journalists who took some photographs and listened to the debriefing. One 76 Squadron crew had been lost, and another struggled in just after Hoover made it home. That was their last flight in BB238 Pinocchio.

After breakfast they cycled back to Beningbrough, and by mid-afternoon they were back in the briefing room at Linton, preparing for another raid. Four times during this tour Jack and the other crew members were detailed for back-to-back operations. The target on 4 April 1943 was Kiel (Op. 47), a target which, in the view of the 76 Squadron ORB compiler, was second only to Hamburg in terms of concentration of shipping and submarines.

The ORB Summary recorded:

> Twelve of our crews helped to make up a strong force of bombers to attack Kiel on the night of 4th April. Only 11 of our aircraft succeeded in reaching the target area. Aircraft 'U' Flight Sergeant Bawden, captain, was compelled to return early to base with the Air Speed Indicator and the artificial horizon unserviceable. Over the entire target area 10/10 cloud persisted and it was therefore impossible for the crews to see the result of their work. The Pathfinders arrived in good time, but even their flares sank into the cloud and were practically of no use to the bomber force. Most of the crews depended on the glow of fires already burning to help then locate the target. The bombs were dropped at heights varying between 17,000 and 20,000ft. The defences over this area were up to their usual strength, and two of our aircraft were slightly damaged. Nevertheless, all our aircraft returned safely.

This was a big raid, with over 550 bombers detailed. Only the two Millennium raids had been bigger. Hoover's crew debriefing suggests that they probably hit the target:

> Attacked primary (target) at 2325 from 19,000ft, located by a green PFF marker seen through cloud. Bombed on estimated position of this marker but own results were not observed.

An entry in 76 Squadron's ORB dated the next day, 5 April 1943, indicates how tight both personnel and matériel resources were on a bomber squadron:

Squadron crew state increased to 14, but serviceability down to 12 (aircraft).

Crew losses could be replaced, and air crew were now emerging from the training bases in some numbers, but they did not have the essential experience necessary for success, and for survival. Aircraft serviceability was dependant on how many hours the technicians and mechanics could work to repair damage and equipment failure. Scheduled maintenance was minimal.

There was another entry in the ORB on 5 April:

Wing Commander Cheshire left the Squadron on posting to Marston Moor as a Group Captain. It was under the direction and personal supervision of Group Captain Cheshire that the Squadron became what it is today – one of the best in Bomber Command. Wing Commander DC Smith took over command.

Leonard Cheshire had commanded 76 Squadron since the beginning of the year. He and Guy Gibson rank as the two most successful squadron commanders in Bomber Command, although they had totally different personalities. Gibson was a straightforward inspirational leader, always in the front with little time for those who would not or could not follow. Cheshire was almost his antithesis of Gibson. Thoughtful and supportive, he was a master of his craft, seeing bombing as a science to be learnt, while making a point of knowing all the people on his squadron, aircrew, ground-crew and administrators alike. Although posted from 76 Squadron on promotion to group captain, Cheshire agitated and argued until he was allowed voluntarily to drop a rank so that he could command 617 Squadron, the squadron which had been formed by Guy Gibson for the dams raid. 617 was now being given a role of attacking special targets, generally requiring very low flying over the target. Unlike Gibson, Cheshire survived the war. One of his last duties was to act as the British observer on the USAAF bomber which dropped an atomic bomb on Nagasaki. He then made a dramatic career change, founding the Cheshire Homes charity.

Whether it had a new compiler, or the new CO just wanted it that way, the squadron's ORB is much richer in its contents from early in April 1943.

Jack's next operation was on 14 April, to Stuttgart (Op. 48). The crew's debriefing was:

> Target identified by PFF flares and visually by built-up area. Bombed on concentration of green markers from 18,000ft at 0109. Several HEs were seen to burst and the target was well alight. At 0103 hours a terrific explosion was observed and two small ones one minute later, believed in NW area. Photo shows fire tracks smoke and gun flashes. Average navigation.

The ORB summary records:

> Ten aircraft were detailed for this raid and each succeeded in penetrating the strong German defences and reaching the target area. Visibility was good and most of the crews were able to visually identify the target. The attack was carried out from an average height of 18,000ft, and as the PFF had been very accurate the results achieved were excellent. Fires, both large and small, were seen to burn all around the aiming point. Several HE bursts were also observed. Of the ten aircraft detailed only one experienced any difficulty regarding the opposition. Aircraft 'W' was attacked by two Ju88s and succeeded in shooting one down. The bomb-aimer, Sergeant Weir on aircraft W was wounded and died later in hospital.

Two nights later, the next operation on 16 April involved a mammoth flight of 9 hours and 45 minutes to Pilsen (Op. 49), to bomb the Skoda factory. The intention was to complete the destruction of the Skoda works following previous visits by Bomber Command. The 76 Squadron ORB records:

> 11 crews were detailed to attack Pilsen, and one to Mannheim. Both Attacks were highly successful. Over Pilsen the railway, factory, and river could be visually identified. The defences around the Skoda factory were also helped by the weather and the flak was very accurate. Three aircraft failed to return.

Sergeant Wedderburn's crew in aircraft 'E' were reported missing as were the crews of Sergeant Webb and Sergeant Wright.

Sergeant Hickman jettisoned his bombs twenty miles off Skegness because the rear gun turret was unserviceable.

Hoover's crew reported:

> Attacked primary target from 9,000ft at 0151. Target identified by loop in river South of target and bombed on estimated distances from green ground markers. Many HE explosions concentrated probably to the South end of the target. Photo shows ground detail and incendiary tracks. Good navigation.

The Pilsen raid cost Bomber Command thirty-six aircraft and their crews – an attrition rate of 11 per cent. It was also an unsuccessful raid, despite the reports in the squadron ORB. Air Marshal Harris recorded in his book *Bomber Offensive*[11] that the bombing concentration was remarkably good for so distant a target, but the main force had been misled by Pathfinder markers placed over a mile from the aiming point. Max Hastings[12] adds that the Pathfinders had marked a lunatic asylum at Dobrany believing it to be the Skoda factory. Bomber Command's overall losses on this raid amounted to 11 per cent of the attacking force. 76 Squadron bore the brunt of these losses, three aircraft lost out of eleven detailed; an attrition rate of 27 per cent. The one positive aspect of the raid was that the main force of bombers had been accurate in dropping their bombs on the markers. What they needed was someone to tell them whether the markers were in the right place. The role of master bomber, taking tactical command over bomber stream as it reached the target, was still to be fully developed.

The next operation, on 20 April 1943, was a raid on Stettin, then part of Germany but now in Poland (Op. 50). It was something of an experiment as it was the test-piece for new tactics, flying at sea level across the North Sea and Holland.[13] The experiment seemed to work, as all 76 Squadron's aircraft returned, although another squadron lost an aircraft which flew into a windmill. Low level flying was occasionally used again, but the advantage of being below radar cover was offset by the need for more accurate navigation. The report from Hoover's crew was:

> Target located by PFF green markers and visually by

waterways and built-up area. Bombed on green markers from 15,000ft at 0115, and own bombs seen to burst in built-up area...terrific explosion observed at 0125.

Then it was back to the Ruhr on 26 April, to bomb Duisberg (Op. 51). The ORB record of Hoover's crew debrief states:

Attacked primary at 0250 from 18,000ft. Located red and green markers. Concentrated mass of fire 3 miles in diameter. Photo show intense fire tracks.

The ORB summary is succinct:

10 aircraft in raid – all returned.

This was the time when it could be said, with hindsight, that Bomber Command was winning the Battle of the Ruhr. However, Jack and the rest of Hoover's crew had nearly completed their part in the battle. On 28 April they did a gardening operation in the Kategat off Anholt Island (Op. 52). Their crew debrief states:

Mines dropped as ordered at midnight from 3000ft. Both parachutes were seen to open.

A little nonchalant perhaps. But two days later, on 30 April 1943, they were over Essen again (Op. 53) for the fourth time in this tour, and the raid did not go so well. The ORB summary gives details:

12 aircraft were detailed for the raid. One became 'bogged', and another became too late for take-off. This the start of a 'none too good a night'. On the way to target another two were compelled to turn back, one with GEE and DR Compass unserviceable, and the other with loss of airspeed indicator. Also encountered was severe icing. Another disappointment still met the Squadron. Sergeant Thomas and crew failed to return from this attack. Consequently, only six are known to have attacked what was believed to be the target. 10/10 cloud prevailed and the Skippers were compelled to depend on the accuracy of the Pathfinders. Only the glow of incendiaries and an occasional HE burst was observed. Some opposition

was encountered and one of our aircraft was hit by light flak but was able to return safely to base.

Getting 'bogged' must have been a very frustrating event. The taxiways to the runway were not all metalled and it was always easy for a pilot to put a wheel on soft ground. It would then take several hours to reduce the aircraft's weight by removing the bombs and then to tug the aircraft out of the mud. Furthermore, a bogged aircraft could prevent others behind it from reaching the runway. Nevertheless, Hoover and his crew seemed to have found the raid worthwhile:

Attacked target at 0255 from 20,000 ft. Red and green tracer markers seen. Bombed on Wanganui TI markers. Glow of incendiaries below cloud.

The Wanganui TI markers were thermal flares which were dropped with parachutes. They were used by the Pathfinders when cloud obscured the ground markers, a tactic known as sky-marking.

And then, suddenly Jack's tour was over, after twenty-two operations. The last one was on 4 May 1943, a relatively short trip to Dortmund (Op. 54). 76 Squadron sent fifteen aircraft on this raid. One (Pilot Officer Bell) failed to return. Hoover's crew debrief simply states:

Attacked at 0215, 18,500 ft. Large explosion seen.

Thirty operations was the nominal length of a tour, but not everyone actually did thirty. 76 Squadron had been in the forefront of the Battle of the Ruhr and had taken many losses. It had been fortunate in having an outstanding commanding officer early in the period, but the aircraft crews, who alone can bring success, had borne the brunt of the battle. Most of Jack's twenty-two operations in 76 Squadron were against the most heavily defended targets, and they were completed in just eleven weeks, an average of one every 3½ days. Unlike the first tour, which had included four relatively safe sea-mining sorties, there was only one such task in this tour. In addition there was a need for air tests to ensure that the aircraft remained serviceable; Jack's log book records fifteen air tests and nine training flights during his time with 76 Squadron, raising the workload to an average of a flying duty every other day. Overall, the aircraft seemed to have been reliable; there was no early return caused by technical defects during this tour.

Jack was posted from 76 Squadron to No. 10 Operational Training Unit on 4 June 1943. With a stand-in wireless operator, Hoover's crew participated in two more raids, and then they had a stroke of luck. So many crews had been lost as they approached the magic figure of thirty that it was decided to screen a few crews from operations earlier than at the normal thirty. It was certainly a morale booster for Hoover's crew, who were screened after twenty-five operations. What other crews thought of the idea does not seem to be recorded.

Hoover was commissioned as an officer in the RCAF and stayed in the UK for another tour, but the other Canadians were posted back to Canada in accordance with their government's policy of only one tour on bombers. The Canadian government had good reason to be wary over the risk to which their airmen were exposed. Writing in *So Many*[14] in 1994, Robert Gale, a Canadian navigator who had joined the RCAF at the age of eighteen, records that of forty-two embryo navigators who crossed the Atlantic together by sea in December 1940 to complete their training at RAF Uxbridge, only four survived their first operational tour. A previous group had not even made it across the Atlantic, having gone down with the liner *Athenia* on the day the war started. The Canadian government never flinched in their support of the UK, but there were some occasions when public opinion required a response.

76 Squadron's part in the Battle of the Ruhr was immense, but it was only one of many squadrons thrown into the battle. Bomber Command had launched 18,506 sorties and lost 872 aircraft, an attrition rate of 4.7 per cent. Fifty-eight thousand tons of bombs had been dropped, mostly on German cities which, as Max Hastings points out,[15] is more than the total dropped by the *Luftwaffe* on the whole of Britain in 1940 and 1941, and more than Bomber Command dropped on the whole of Germany in 1942.

The reward for those 76 Squadron crews who had yet to finish their tour was a highly unpopular move to Home on Spalding Moor, unpopular because Linton was a comfortable base, with permanent buildings and good facilities, and it was within easy reach of York. Home on Spalding Moor, on the other hand, offered only Nissen huts for accommodation, and it was too far away to allow an evening out in York, whilst the nearest town, Market Weighton, was too small to be a satisfactory alternative.

Dissatisfaction with the move was enhanced by the knowledge that RAF Linton-on-Ouse was to be transferred to the RCAF, as were several other airfields in North Yorkshire. The transfers were not, of course, being made just to keep the Canadian crews happy. They were part of a deal agreed between the British and Canadian governments under which the Canadians would provide a complete group of aircraft and aircrew, all expenses paid. Aircraft, crews, training, ordnance, fuel, and all mainte-nance costs would be paid by Canada. The UK's only contribution to the deal was to vacate the North Yorkshire airfields. No. 6 Group RCAF was established at RAF Linton-on-Ouse on 1 January 1943 and in due course it would have two resident RCAF squadrons, No. 408 'Flying Goose' Squadron and No. 426 'Thunderbird' Squadron. Changes such as this are difficult to manage at the best of times, but this one took place in the middle of the bombing campaign, at the height of the Battle of the Ruhr. Beningbrough Hall was now totally requisitioned. A field kitchen was established behind the east wing of the hall, and the whole of the upper two floors were given over to sleeping accommodation.

The population of the village of Nun Monkton began now to see the threat to their small Garden of Eden. *The Story of Nun Monkton*[16] states the problem facing the inhabitants:

Nun Monkton was surrounded by operational airfields including Tockworth, Rufforth, and Clifton. However, it was the base at Linton on Ouse, home to the No. 6 Group squadrons of the Royal Canadian Air force, which adopted Nun Monkton as 'home'. In and around Nun Monkton, the Canadian airmen, when not engaged in bombing raids over Germany, made themselves at home. As alien troops will, whenever billeted on a civilian community, they set about cutting out girl-friends for themselves. They augmented their well-fed charms with ready gifts of luxuries not seen since before the war. They wooed with nylon stockings, with chocolate and other inducements from their richly stocked commissariat. The Nun Monkton men were at a loss. The Canadians were not an enemy occupying force. There could be no question of tarring and feathering a local girl who had succumbed to soft words and Crispy Crunch bars. It was frustrating.

It is tempting to speculate that the author of this extract from the excellent history of Nun Monkton might have been a young resident of the village at the time of the Canadian invasion. As invasions go, however, it was of the beneficial type.

On the face of it, the circumstances were not conducive for an amicable relationship, given the village's lonely location. However, despite an initial coolness, as the war progressed friend-ships were formed, and the villagers absorbed their Canadian guests as their respect for the brave young men grew. The Alice Hawthorn was the catalyst in this development, with Ted Dodman and his wife offering the home comforts of good food and a family atmosphere, which the airmen had left thousands miles away. A nine verse poem penned by the Canadian airmen illustrates the success of the Dodman's efforts; a copy still hangs in the pub's bar. The author of *The Story of Nun Monkton* notes that the poem carries more sincerity than metric felicity. As we are losing track of both Jack and Hoover's crew, I will offer only one verse here, but I will re-produce the whole poem at Appendix 3, because for me, for all its roughness, it illustrates exactly the values shared at that time by the British and Canadian people; values which carried Jack through three operational tours.

> The lads who come here again and again,
> They've no inclination to roam,
> They know very well that "The Alice" is swell
> They look upon it as home

Enough of rustic poetry; but before we lose sight of Jack Mossop and the Canadian-dominated crew with which he completed his second tour, it is worth stopping to consider the enormous contribution to the bombing campaign made by airmen from Canada, Australia and New Zealand. John Terraine points out[17] that in January 1943, 37 per cent of all Bomber Command pilots came from the three countries, and of these 55 per cent were from Canada. Some of the Canadian pilots actually came from the USA, joining as volunteers. These figures exclude RCAF pilots posted to UK to serve in No. 6 Group.

The juxtaposition of British and Canadian aircrew led to some interesting debate over issues on which the RAF can be somewhat coy. More so than the other armed forces, the distinction between commissioned and non-commissioned personnel can be difficult to determine simply by considering what they do. The pilot of a bomber has overall responsibility for getting to the target and back, and most might see it as a job which carries sufficient responsibility to require a commissioned officer for the task. Yet many crews had a sergeant as pilot and one or more commissioned officers in other roles. The RAF has often had to debate the issue with its colleagues in the British Army and the Royal Navy, not always reaching agreement. The debate is usually based on leadership. The rear gunner and the wireless operator in a bomber crew have to be skilled and brave enough to see to their tasks when under fire, but they may not require the leadership qualities required of a pilot. The RAF argued that it is the capacity to lead which should determine who should be commissioned. However, the RCAF, backed up by Australian and New Zealand air forces, saw difficulties in having a mix of commissioned and non-commissioned officers in a crew. They argued that all members of a crew share the same risk. Furthermore, when off-duty, aircrew should be able to socialise and to live as a team, which they cannot do if they have to use different messes. They therefore favoured all-commissioned crews. The debate still sometimes emerges, but in 1942 the RAF's view prevailed, if only because the RAF had a great preponderance of operational aircrew, and there were more important issues to deal with.

By now the RAF was no longer alone in taking the fight to the enemy. In addition to the contributions from the dominion air forces, the USA had manufactured and brought into service a large fleet of Boeing Fortress bombers (generally called the Flying Fortress) which were flung into the conflict in mass daylight bombing raids. The range of targets which the RAF and the USAAF were instructed to attack widened at this stage, to include railway centres, ports and submarine bases as well as cities. The Allies were also beginning to see some success on the ground. The Russians had re-gained some ground along the front of over 1,000 miles which divided their armies from the Germans. In Tunisia the British Army was winning tank battles against German and Italian opposition, and the victory at El Alamein was at last being exploited. Success in North Africa led to a fifth meeting between Winston Churchill and President Roosevelt, following which planning for an invasion of the German-held European mainland began. On 9 July 1943 the Allies invaded Sicily.

When we last saw Jack Mossop, he was heading towards No. 10 Operational Training Unit at RAF Abingdon, a few miles south of Oxford, where new aircrew were trained using Whitley aircraft. He was there for only one month, instructing on radio systems. On 14 July 1943 he was posted to No. 1664 Conversion Unit (1664 CU) Croft, near Darlington. Croft was by then one of the bases managed by the RCAF as part of No. 6 Group, although it is now better known as a motor racing circuit. In December 1943, as part of the changes necessary for the establishment of No. 6 Group RCAF, 1664 CU moved a few miles south down the A1 to RAF Dishforth, the airfield where Jack's brother Bill had been fatally injured in a Wellington bomber six months previously. Jack's job was wireless operator training, but on two occasions he was in a Halifax detailed to conduct a sea search for a dinghy; hopefully the dinghies would have contained living aircrew. While he was at Dishforth, Jack's first DFC was announced in the London Gazette, on 17 August 1943, alongside the announcement of the same award for his 76 Squadron pilot, the newly commissioned Pilot Officer Hoover. Jack's citation is not recorded, but Hoover's can be taken as a measure of the whole crew's bravery:

This officer has completed many operational sorties, several of which have been against the most heavily defended German targets, including Hamburg, Berlin, and the Ruhr Valley. He has secured some excellent photographs and has displayed great skill as a captain of aircraft, whilst the discipline and efficiency of his crew is of the highest order. Pilot Officer Hoover has performed his duties resolvedly with great determination and in the face of heavy opposition has invariably shown praiseworthy courage and coolness.

Leave was not seen as essential as it was on a front-line unit, but there were some opportunities, and it is only forty-five miles from Dishforth to Durham City, up the A1 Great North Road. Even as a commissioned officer, Jack's favoured mode of transport was hitchhiking. The A1 trunk road was (and still is) the way home for many inhabitants of County Durham and Northumberland. It is no coincidence that many bomber airfields were built alongside the A1 during the Second World War. An essential ingredient of a bomber offensive is bombs. The bomb depots of the bomber bases had to be re-stocked on a daily basis. Easy access from a trunk road or in some cases a railway branch line was essential to the campaign. Each night lorries carrying many hundreds of bombs destined to be dropped on enemy territory stocked up the bomb depots at the airfields. Hitch-hiking was the normal mode of transport for servicemen travelling to and from leave, although officers were not supposed to travel in such a manner. For journeys along the Great North Road it was a reliable mode of travel.

One day, on reaching Durham courtesy of A1 drivers, Jack dropped into the bar of the Three Tuns Hotel for a glass of beer. Seeing him standing alone at the bar, the landlord introduced him to a young lady who was staying at the hotel. It was Hilda Charlton, come down from Medomsley for the weekend. The Three Tuns belonged to the parents of a school friend, and she was allowed occasionally to stay in Durham overnight. Hilda was working for a timber importing company in Newcastle upon Tyne. Wood was an essential war commodity, and the routes taken by ships bringing timber to Britain were kept secret. Medomsley is about ten miles from Newcastle, and she commuted by bus, about thirty minutes each way, except when she was on duty as a volunteer fire watcher. The office building was in the centre of the city, and it was taller than others in the street. Its roof provided a good platform for observing any fires started by bombing raids. As it happened, the *Luftwaffe* did not target Newcastle on the nights when Hilda was on fire watch duty, so she did not experience at first hand the immediate impact of a bombing campaign, although she did see the damage when the *Luftwaffe* caused considerable disruption in the area around Manors railway station close to her office building.

In the bleak years of war, when few luxuries existed, and few could afford them anyway, the dance hall provided the main form of entertainment, and the Three Tuns had an excellent dance floor. Hilda was an accomplished and enthusiastic dancer. Unfortunately, Jack could not dance at all, and he had no intention of learning. The best Hilda could manage was to get him to sit and watch others do the dancing.

Nevertheless, Hilda and Jack must have got on well enough, because by the end of 1943 they were engaged to be married. Their courtship would have seemed risible by today's society. They would meet about once a month for a few hours, and they would have had little opportunity to be alone together. Jack's powers of determination were evident from his exploits, although Hilda would have known little of them. She was also of a determined personality, and both seem to have shared the virtue of patience. The means by which they became engaged was later (much later) told to me by Hilda. Jack had managed a short period of home leave and as usual they had met up at the Three Tuns. Before he returned to Dishforth Jack gave Hilda £20 – a lot of money in those days, the equivalent of £600 in 2006. With it she was to purchase a ring from the Northern Goldsmiths, a well known jewellery shop in Newcastle. What she did not know was that on 9 October 1943 Jack had at last received the £30 bounty which comes with a DFM. Towards the end of the following week Jack appeared at Hilda's workplace, and he invited her to accompany him to the tea room in one of Newcastle's best hotels, where in an ambience of appropriate of luxury he took the ring from her and placed it on her finger, asking for her hand in marriage as he did so. On gaining her acceptance he escorted his fiancée back to her office building. He then hitchhiked back to Dishforth.

Jack seems to have approached the business of courting as an extension of his day job. Find the target, achieve concentration, and – above all – assume success. Once his mind was made up on any issue, he assumed that others would go along with him. In this case, Hilda was not at all fazed by the implication that, in buying the engagement ring, she had already indicated that she would accept Jack's proposal. Their relationship was based on a simple mutual understanding that they were meant for each other. And in their time together there was no breach of that under-standing. As a love story, theirs was too simple and unbroken to be remarkable, except of course that Jack was required to spend most of his time away from Hilda, working in the high risk business of wartime military flying, and that he still had another tour of operations to complete; a tour which would entail thirty-six more bombing raids over enemy territory.

Jack did not have to do another tour; only volunteers could be posted for a third tour. He had lost two brothers on war duties during the previous six months. His eldest brother, Harry, had been killed in action in Greece in July, and as noted above, Bill Mossop had been killed at Dishforth in June. Bill was the closest to Jack in age, and the one with whom he played rugby for their school. Jack could have honourably decided that the war had taken a sufficient toll from the Mossop family. But when Hoover and the British contingent of Pinocchio's crew turned up at Dishforth for their Lancaster conversion training, it did not take him long to volunteer. The formation of the Pathfinder squadrons was distorting the experience range across Bomber Command, and a volunteer with two operational tours could not be ignored.

1. Jack Mossop's father, Joe, with two of his sons Arthur and Joe junior.

2. Jack Mossop's eldest brother, Harry, in army uniform.

3. Four brothers in uniform, left to right: Jack, Harry, Joe and Bill, probably photographed in August 1941 when Jack is known to have had a week's leave.

4. Grace Mossop in WAAF uniform.

5. Bill Mossop during his night fighter tour in Blenheims.

6. Hampden AD797 at Scampton. This was the aircraft written off after crash landing at Bircham Newton when returning from a raid on Cuxhaven airfield (Op. 27), in which Jack won his DFM.

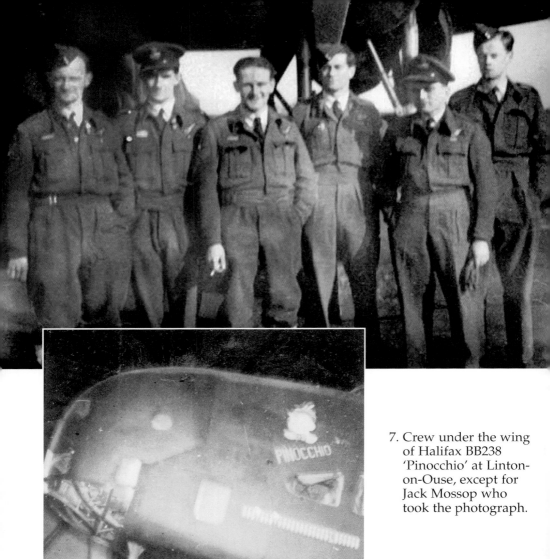

7. Crew under the wing of Halifax BB238 'Pinocchio' at Linton-on-Ouse, except for Jack Mossop who took the photograph.

8. 'Pinocchio' in a hangar at Linton for repairs after the raid on Essen on 3 April 1943 (Op. 46).

9. Beningbrough Hall photographed in 2006. Hoover's crew were billeted on the top floor.

10. The Alice Hawthorn pub photographed in 2006.

11. Remains of the ferry landing used to gain access across the River Ouse to the Alice Hawthorn.

12. Jack and Hilda on their wedding day.

13. Wedding guests.

14. Flight Lieutenant
    Hoover, pilot.

15. Flight Sergeant
Jock MacKenzie,
air gunner.

16. Flight Sergeant
Cliff Hill, air
gunner.

17. Flight Lieutenant Mossop in No 1 uniform.

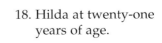

18. Hilda at twenty-one years of age.

Mon. Night of 5-6 June.

5 It became rather obvious during the day and at Ops. Briefing that this was IT. We were to bomb COASTAL BATTERIES at MAISY on French coast. A late take-off 0135. On way out saw

Tues. Gliders towers and troops carrying

6 a/c formating. We bombed precisely on A/P also marked it and saw "invasion fleet" on way back. A quiet trip for us but the beginning of great things.

Wed. 6th – 7th Deputy Master Bomber on an

7 important road centre town through which Jerry reserves were coming. St LÔ in Normandy. Cloudy all way and over Δ – we bombed rather low level. Our Markers close to A/P and bombs "bang on". Good photograph.

Thur. *Corpus Christi* 8-9th June.

8 D.M.B. again at another communications centre at MAYENNE, south of the battle front. Weather was awful – Thick cloud and rain all the way but, amazingly, it was clear over target

Fri. Right on the A/P with markers

9 and bombs and got another good photo'. On way back saw activity on "Second Front". Dreadful landing conditions – cloud down to 100' and heavy rain. Was complimented by C.O. for recent raids.

Sat.

10 On Leave.

Sun. *1st after Trinity*

11

Memo.

19. Extract from diary 5 to 11 June 1944.

20. Extract from diary 7 to 13 August 1944.

Mon. *Bank Holiday*

7

Tues. Did a' one man P.F.F. job tonight.

8 Supposed to be D.M.B. but M/8 had trouble and didn't take off so we took over. Impossible to see ground in D area so we dropped flares and came in again to mark A/P accurately with Green T.I. Then

Wed. we directed bombing

9 which was very good – well-concentrated. A tremendous explosion at +6 and burning still visible when we were 80 miles away. Target, by the way, was Petrol and Oil dump at AIRE-sur-LYS.

Thur. (only 90th)

10 On Leave.

Fri. ☾

11

Sat.

12

Sun. *10th after Trinity*

13

Memo.

21. Photograph of daylight raid on V1 launch site at Marquise, near Calais (Op. 79).

22. Jack and Hilda Mossop, Jack's sister Mary, and the author apparent as a bump in my mother's coat, outside Buckingham Palace after Jack had received his two DFCs.

23. Jack, Hilda and young Bill outside Stags Head cottage, Medomsley.

24. Dance invitation.

The Officer Commanding and Officers,

R.A.F. Station, Ossington

request the pleasure of the company of

Mrs J. Mossop

to a Mess Dance

on Saturday, 26th May 1945.

at 8 p.m.

R.S.V.P. to
Mess Secretary
R.A.F. Station, Ossington
Newark, Notts.

Dress optional

25. Beach party at Branksome Chine, Bournemouth.

26. Tel Aviv Officers' Club 14 February 1946. Two of Jack's companions are Captain Holdaway and First Officer Pete Harding but it is not known which is which.

TO FLIGHT RADIO OFFICER

FROM R/o MOSSOP

R/o BLADES

LANC. TRAINING FLIGHT
G.AGMF — 20 AUG. 1946.

TELEGRAPHY — FAIR
LOG-KEEPING — POOR
KNOWLEDGE OF ROUTE — INCOMPLETE

The above-named R/o was quite keen, and, as he gets more experience, should be efficient. At present his faults are; slowness, an incomplete knowledge of facilities available and a lamentable habit of trying to hold lots of stuff in his head and filling up his log at his leisure. He seems slowly to be overcoming this.

27. Notes on Radio
Officer Blades.

ROYAL AIR FORCE

PATH FINDER FORCE

Award of
Path Finder Force Badge

This is to certify that

FLYING OFFICER J. MOSSOP, D.F.C., D.F.M. 14416

having qualified for the award of the Path Finder Force Badge, an

having now completed satisfactorily the requisite conditions o

operational duty in the Path Finder Force, is hereby

Permanently awarded the Path Finder Force Badg

Issued this 15th ~ day of AUGUST in the year 19**44**.

Air Officer Commanding, Path Finder Force

28. Path Finder Badge
Certificate.

29. Jack with his son on the bridge which leads to Branksome Chine, Bournemouth.

30. Hilda with Bill Lloyd at Bath, on the way home to Bournemouth following Cliff Hill's wedding in Oswestry.

31. Hilda and Bill Lloyd in July 2006, their first meeting since 1946.

RADIO OFFICER
J. MOSSOP DFC & BAR DFM
BRITISH OVERSEAS AIRWAYS
CORPORATION
20TH AUGUST 1946   AGE 26

REMEMBERED ALWAYS

32. Jack's grave in Bernay Cemetery.

Chapter 9

Pathfinding

The development of bombing tactics during the strategic bombing offensive was almost entirely based on the development of new technology. Whilst it is true that the introduction of bigger aircraft with more powerful engines able to carry heavier bombs greatly increased the capability of Bomber Command, it was the developments in electronic navigation and bombing technology which most influenced the development of bombing tactics. Before looking at Pathfinder tactics, we should consider the impact of these technological developments because without them the Pathfinder Force could not have been successful.

From its start in 1939 the Second World War was a contest of scientific and technological development as well as a trial of strength, leadership, and courage. Nowhere was this contest more closely fought than in the development of electronic devices to improve the accuracy of navigation of bomber aircraft and, from the defenders' point of view, the detection, interception and destruction of those bombers. The constant factor which generated this contest was darkness. Not until the last phase of the war, when enemy defences were worn down, could the USAAF mount regular daylight raids over Germany, and then only with long range fighter aircraft escort. The need to fly in the dark spurred the British research establishments – primarily the Telecommunications Research Establishment (TRE) – to develop and put into production an array of radar and other devices which exploited the electromagnetic spectrum.

During his first tour, Jack's tools of the trade as a wireless operator amounted to two radio systems, one operating in the high frequency (HF) band and one in the very high frequency band (VHF). Above or close to the UK, radio-telephony (RT) enabled speech between aircraft and ground bases using VHF frequencies. Further away from base HF wireless telegraphy (WT) enabled communication using the Morse code. Navigation at night often relied on dead reckoning, which was accurate only if the direction and strength of the wind was known, and on astro-navigation, using a sextant to determine the aircraft's position from the positions of stars. If the stars were not visible because of high cloud, accurate navigation was possible only by flying low enough to see landmarks on the ground, with the moon as the only light source. When the ground could not be seen, navigators had to rely on dead reckoning, using a compass and a watch, to set a course to a target. To obtain the navigational accuracy required even to find cities, never mind bomb them, the navigator's dead reckoning and his awkward charts had to be removed from the process. Enter the boffins.

The first electronic navigation aid available to Bomber Command was GEE, an acronym of Ground Electronic Engineering. The naming of such devices is in itself a sign of the times. Security considerations dictated that a name of an electronic system should not reveal its purpose, which gave ample opportunity to scientists to stretch their imagination when naming their inventions. GEE had a rather neutral name when compared with later devices but it did have a ground element, consisting of three static radio transmitting stations spread many miles apart in England. The transmitters simultaneously emitted a series of timed pulses. When received by an aircraft the pulses were no longer simultaneous because the distances from each transmitter to the aircraft would differ. The time differences enabled the navigator to calculate the location of the aircraft using a special set of charts. So the navigator still had to carry charts, and positions still had to be plotted manually in the aircraft. The system was also vulnerable to jamming. The German air defence system soon deployed jamming transmitters which restricted the effective range of GEE, so that at times it became of more use to aircraft returning to base than a means of finding the target. The best means of overcoming jamming was to increase the power of the signal received by the bombers, and the best way to do that was to reduce the distance from the ground transmitter to the aircraft. Mobile GEE transmitters were therefore built and were shipped to Normandy as soon as the D-Day landings had established a safe route inland.[1]

TRE then developed a system in which the calculations were made on the ground rather than in the air. The Oboe system was a blind bombing device which we have already noted in Chapter 8.

On 5 March 1944, Jack was in a Halifax in the main force attacking the Krupps munitions factory at Essen, when Oboe was used for the first time. Two transmitters in the south of England sent out pulses of radio energy which were received by a high-flying Mosquito aircraft, amplified and sent back. One of the Oboe ground stations, known as cat, calculated the distance to the aircraft by measuring the time between transmitting a pulse and receiving the response. Instructions sent to the pilot caused the aircraft, as it approached the target, to fly in a circular course centred on one of the two ground stations. The circular course almost passed over the target. The second ground station, called mouse, would send an instruction which would cause the aircraft to drop its bombs or, more likely, its aiming point marker flares. Allowance had to be made for the circular motion of the aircraft, which would cause the markers to veer off at a tangent, which is why the circular course did not take the aircraft directly over the aiming point.

Oboe was very accurate. R.V. Jones notes[2] that it was so accurate that scientists had to consider the accuracy of alignment of the UK Ordnance Survey with mapping systems on the continent. They gave the system its name during the experimental stage of its development; apparently the transmitter aerial hummed with a sound reminiscent of an oboe. The disadvantage of Oboe was that only one aircraft could use it at a time, but one accurate marker on the aiming point was often all that was needed.

In June 1944, an improved version of GEE, known as GEE (H), was introduced, which gave it the same accuracy as Oboe, but with the further benefit of enabling more than one aircraft to use the system. In the meantime Bomber Command needed a device which told the aircrew in the bombing stream where they were, and more particularly when they were over the target, particularly when cloud or smoke prevented visual sighting.

The solution was an on-board ground mapping radar which would present a picture of the landscape directly below the aircraft. The solution was based on one of the most famous of all British wartime inventions, the cavity magnetron valve. The magnetron became the source of energy for radar systems in many different roles, on land, sea and air. Energy reflected back from the ground, from ships, from aircraft, and even from the snorkel of a submarine could be used to provide a constantly updating picture. How best to exploit this invention caused much debate. The Battle of the Atlantic was in full flow at the time when the radar was becoming ready for deployment and an ability to find snorkelling submarines could tip the balance in favour of the Allies. Furthermore, if an aircraft equipped with a magnetron radar was shot down over the sea, the secret of the magnetron would not be compromised, whilst an aircraft shot down over Germany would reveal the capability of the invention. The argument continued during the usual delays in developing new equipment and then in the establishment of production lines. The technical difficulties caused the scientists to name the radar H2S, the chemical formula for hydrogen sulphide – a very smelly gas. When a senior manager queried the name, a bright young scientist quickly saved embarrassment by saying that H2S was an abbreviation of 'Home Sweet Home', which none could gainsay. In the event, it was agreed that Bomber Command had priority over Coastal Command for the first radar sets. Halifax V 9977 is credited as the first bomber to have the H2S radar system fitted, and the radar was first used by Pathfinders in a raid on Hamburg on 3 January 1943.

The last operational use of H2S radar, albeit in a much advanced version than Jack had used, was during the brief Falklands War when Vulcan bombers, themselves about to be withdrawn from service, flew five operations in support of the British Task Force sent to recover the Falklands following an invasion by Argentina. In the first of these raids, on 1 May 1982, Flight Lieutenant Martin Withers and his crew of Vulcan 607 dropped a string of twenty 1,000 lb bombs which closed the runway at Port Stanley to fast jet aircraft, thus gaining British air superiority over the Falkland Islands, and severely the limiting the ability of the Argentine air force to attack the ships of the British Task Force.[3] The H2S radar set in a Vulcan was much more powerful and more capable than those which the Pathfinders had used forty years previously, but the basic design of a rotating aerial pointing downwards, both emitting powerful pulses of radio energy and receiving the much weaker echoes reflected back from the ground or ships on the sea had not changed.

Radar was almost made for the Second World War. Although often thought to be a British invention, it was a German, Heinrich Hertz who, in 1886, first demonstrated a radar device when he showed that radio waves could bounce back off metallic surfaces. In 1904, another German, Hulsmeyer, experimented with radio waves bouncing back off the sides of ships. Subsequent development work was mainly in the USA, at the Naval Research Laboratory. Although the US Navy was more active in developing radar systems, the United States Army Signal Corp was sufficiently advanced to have six long range search radars in Hawaii at the time of the attack on Pearl Harbor in December 1941. One of the radars detected the Japanese attack, but the significance of the blips on the operator's display was ignored. British interest in the military use of radar began in the 1930s, initially into the feasibility of generating radio death rays.[4] A more likely use of radio waves was developed instead, that of detecting aircraft in flight beyond the reach of the human eye and ear. By 1938 the Chain Home radar stations had been built around the south and east coasts of England. Chain Home was crucial to the result of the Battle of Britain. Although it started later, the *Luftwaffe* soon developed its own radar chain for air defence. British Intelligence staff named it the Kammhuber Line after the German general who was in charge of air defence. General Kammhuber was later flattered to find that the radar chain had been named after him; nobody in Germany had considered such a title. Kammhuber was one of the few German generals to maintain a military career after the war, holding appointments in NATO and becoming the German Chief of Air Staff.[5]

Radar was soon being used by all combatants on land, at sea, and in the air. Both sides knew, however, that all radar systems then available could be blinded by a simple defensive measure. Small metallic strips, cut to the wavelengths of the radars which were to be blinded, were dropped from aircraft, creating a reflective curtain which took many hours to dissipate. This highly effective radar countermeasure was first known as Window in the RAF, but it was later called chaff. Although both the RAF and the *Luftwaffe* knew about its potential, neither dared to use it for fear that the other would also. Eventually, however, the balance of risk turned as the benefit to Bomber Command became significantly greater than the disadvantage of disruption of the British defensive radar systems. Window was first used on 24 July 1943 during the firestorm raid on Hamburg. Although the chaff partially blinded the H2S radar on RAF bombers, the benefits of blinding the Kammhuber line and other German air defence radar systems more than justified its deployment.

The constant application of new technology, and the upgrading of that already delivered, was a significant factor in the success of Bomber Command. New aircraft types with more powerful and more reliable engines enabled the crews to put heavier bombs on more distant targets. But it was the less well understood discipline of electronic engineering that finally provided the accuracy in both navigation and bomb-aiming which was necessary for an effective bomber offensive. Not the least advantageous was a new bomb-sight. Early bomb-sights were little more than a fixed mesh which the bomb-aimer looked through over the target area, releasing the bombs when the target was in a specific part of the grid. The big disadvantage of such a simple bomb-sight was the aircraft had to be held in straight and level flight during the approach to the target. The Mark XIV was an electronic device which enabled the bomb-aimer to release the bombs when not in straight and level flight – a major advance in survivability, as the pilot could weave on the approach. It also improved accuracy as there was less incentive to release bombs early. This was such an advance that the new sight was deemed to be 'all singing all dancing'.

A consequence of these advances in technology was an erosion of the distinction between the roles of navigator, bomb-aimer, and wireless operator in a heavy bomber. H2S, for instance, was used primarily as navigation aid, but it in some conditions it could provide a clear map of the target, invaluable to the bomb-aimer. In a Lancaster, the H2S equipment was installed in a rack on the port side of the fuselage, some distance from the bomb-aimer's forward position from where he would release the bombs. Crew cooperation had always been important in bombers; now it became essential.

A dozen or more different types of electronic equipment might be fitted to a heavy bomber. 'Boozer', for instance, was a passive device which alerted the pilot if the aircraft was being scanned by an enemy radar transmitter. If the radar was one of the ground-based Wurzburg gun-layers, an orange light appeared on a panel in the pilot's cockpit; if it was a red light it meant that a fighter with Lichtenstein radar was on his tail – the response taken by the pilot would depend on which colour illuminated. Monica was a rear-facing radar which provided warning of an attack by enemy fighters, although in doing so it could also give away the bomber's own position. Mandrel was a device used to jam the German air defence Freya radar used by the German air defence system, but by 1943 it had become largely ineffective because of modifications to the Freya radars. It was not only the radar systems which were the target of what we would now call electronic countermeasure systems. Tinsel was a device which a bomber wireless operator could use to jam the German fighter control broadcast frequency. Airborne Cigar (ABC) was another radio jamming device, switched on only for a few minutes at a time to avoid drawing too much attention. Some devices, such as a radar seeking device called Serrate, were fitted only in Beaufighter and Mosquito aircraft which, by 1944, were regularly flying with the bombers. There was, however, one deception system which needed no more than a radio. A 'Special Wireless Operator' was a German-speaking linguist who gave false information to the German air defence ground controllers. Many of these special operators were Jews who had escaped from Germany ahead of the Nazi purges.

In addition to the devices carried by the bombers, from the beginning of 1944, Boeing B-17 Mark III Fortresses of RAF No. 100 Group provided specialised electronic countermeasures to protect the bombing squadrons. One of these devices was a huge radio device known as Jostle which could jam all the *Luftwaffe*'s

VHF radio frequencies from 38 to 42 megacycles. It was used on a sporadic basis for about two minutes at a time. This was so successful that the German ground controllers had to resort to the use of commercial radio transmitters from which they broadcast certain types of music to tell the night-fighter pilots which cities were being attacked. The Fortresses flew about 2,000 feet above the main force, five or six aircraft spaced out above the bombing stream.[6]

New technology made a tremendous contribution to the effectiveness of Bomber Command, but it required additional training of the crews who had to operate the various devices, and it required even greater teamwork. In particular, the roles of navigators, bomb-aimers and the wireless operators became less distinct. In the Pathfinder squadrons, it was often necessary to increase the crew complement to eight to ensure that all the necessary skills were available.

The success of the Pathfinders relied also on a remarkable aircraft. It would usually be acknowledged that the three best products of British aircraft manufacturers during the Second World War were the Spitfire, the Lancaster, and the Mosquito. It is more difficult to agree which of the three was the most successful. The German view was clear: the Mosquito caused them the most difficulty. Too fast for their fighters to catch, and too manoeuvrable even for radar-directed anti-aircraft guns, the Mosquito was a formidable bomber, unable to carry the bomb-load of the heavy bombers, but more able to survive and fight another day.

Sharing Graveley with 35 Squadron's Lancasters was 692 Squadron which was equipped with a special version of the Mosquito, the Mark IX. Their two Merlin engines gave the aircraft a maximum speed of 380mph, and it could reach an altitude of 36,000ft. The Mk XI could carry four 500lb bombs, but its most important ordnance were the flares which marked the aiming point within the target area. Flying ahead of the Pathfinders' Lancasters, safe from all ground-to-air cannon fire and from hostile night-fighters, Mosquitoes used the cat and mouse signals of the Oboe blind bombing system to place the first markers of the raid.

Jack never flew in a Mosquito, but he would have known all

about them, and on one occasion he flew in formation with one on a daylight raid, as we shall soon see.

As we have noted already in this account of the bombing campaign, the concept of a master bomber was used almost spontaneously by Guy Gibson during the Dams raid in May 1943. However, Gibson had the advantage of Very High Frequency (VHF) radios, borrowed from Fighter Command and installed in 617 Squadron Lancasters especially for the Dams raid. This gave Gibson radio telephony speech communication with his squadron over the target area. 617 Squadron was retained in a specialist role after their exploits over the dams. Along with others squadrons in No. 5 Group, they explored and developed the concept of the master bomber in attacks on small targets of high military significance, usually requiring great accuracy. Perhaps the most notable example being an attack in June 1943 on a factory which manufactured radar components at Friedrichshafen, on the German shore of Lake Constance. The attack was controlled by a senior officer using VHF air-to-air radio. The technique later became intrinsic to Pathfinder tactics, perhaps most famously in the raid on the V-weapon development site at Peenemunde in July 1943, when Pathfinders from No. 8 Group provided the master bomber. However, the technique could not be used generally until the Pathfinder and the main force aircraft were all fitted with VHF radios, a process not complete until well into the summer of 1943. By the time Jack Mossop became a Pathfinder in 1944, the use of master bombers for tactical control over the target had become standard. A master bomber aircraft circling the target area would observe the locations of the flares and determine the best approach to the aiming point. The Pathfinder aircraft of No. 8 Group would bomb first, starting fires through a mix of ordnance. The main force of bombers would be guided to a well lit target and take tactical instructions from the PFF master bomber. If necessary, the master bomber would call for more markers (or target indicators) which he might drop himself. The role of master bomber required his own aircraft to stay in the target area for longer than the other bombers, significantly increasing the risk of being shot down. A second crew, the deputy master bomber, was therefore tasked to take over the role if required. Although a master bomber and his deputy were nominally the pilots of the designated aircraft, his crew shared the responsibility, and the increased risk.

By the time Jack joined 76 Squadron in February 1943 the principle of concentration had been proven; bombing did most damage if it was concentrated on a small area. The tactics required to apply the concept had been developed, and all bombers attacking targets in Germany had been fitted with GEE. This was a big step forward, but the value of GEE was more in general navigation than as a targeting device. It would help find the target, but it could not put a crew over the aiming point. To some degree GEE failed to live up to expectations, but knowing what it could do was crucial to the development of Pathfinder tactics. The idea that a few aircraft, equipped with the latest navigation equipment and manned by the most experienced crews, could lead the main force of bombers to a target was tested in exercises held in Wales early in 1942, using the prototype of GEE. The tactics adopted, following this exercise, split the Pathfinder bombers into three groups: illuminators, target markers and followers. The illuminators were the first to reach the target, and they marked it with incendiaries. The markers then dropped a line of flares to show the way to the target. The rest of the Pathfinders, the followers, then illuminated the target with flares. If cloud or smoke hid the target, aerial flares with parachutes were dropped to guide the main force bombers which arrived after the Pathfinders. The first trial of the technique was against Essen on 8 March 1942; but neither it, nor the two subsequent trials, were especially successful. However, with refinement and practice Pathfinder tactics soon became the standard for the strategic bombing offensive.

After some debate, and against the initial view of Air Marshal Harris at Bomber Command, it was determined that special squadrons should be formed with the best crews in Bomber Command. A new Group, No. 8, was formed under the command of Air Commodore Don Bennett to act as a Pathfinder Force. Initially some of the best crews and most successful squadrons were transferred into the new group, to the consternation of the other group commanders, but as their tactics evolved the Pathfinders were seen as a special rather than an elite group.

When the Pathfinders were formed in No. 8 Group in August 1942, Air Marshal Harris had insisted that the most proficient crews were posted to the Pathfinder squadrons, but these were the crews who could have expected quick promotion in their current squadron, at least up to squadron leader rank. Furthermore, Pathfinder crews would carry more risk exposure because of the need to stay longer in the target area. Harris therefore declared that that Pathfinder aircrew would be given accelerated promotion, and they were given a distinguishing badge in the form of an eagle, to be worn below the aircrew brevet. These manifestations of elitism did not go down well with the squadron commanders who were required to offer up their best crews. A squadron's effectiveness was measured mainly by its position on the bombing ladder maintained by Bomber Command Headquarters. It was based on the photographs taken automatically when the crews dropped their bombs. There was an obvious temptation to offer the less effective crews to the Pathfinders. To counter this temptation, the Air Officer Commanding No. 8 Group, Air Commodore Don Bennett, turned to one of Bomber Command's most decorated and charismatic pilots, Hamish Mahaddie, who one day in February 1943 had been to Buckingham Palace to receive four medals at a single investiture: a DSO, a DFC, a DFM, and a Czech Military Cross. Mahaddie became the Pathfinder's Group Training Officer. He regularly flew on operations with the Pathfinder squadrons, but his main job was to ensure that only the best crews became Pathfinders. He developed a technique of arriving at a bomber base just as the photographs of the previous night's target were becoming available, and he quickly identified the crews he wanted. He also found ways of recognising the weaker crews which squadron commanders tried to send to the Pathfinders. Mahaddie became known as 'Bennett's horse thief'. However, not all Pathfinder crews were taken from operational squadrons. Once the initial surge was over, many were taken directly from the training units. Mahaddie himself acknowledged the quality of new aircrew arriving from the Commonwealth Air Training Scheme, which we came across in Chapter 4.[7] Nevertheless, in March 1944 a posting to a Pathfinder squadron was still seen as recognition of high competence in the increasingly technical art of bombing.

In April 1944, Flying Officer Jack Mossop DFC DFM was posted to the Navigating Training Unit of No. 8 (Pathfinder) Group, at RAF Upwood, another airfield in the flat land between Peterborough and Huntingdon. Hoover, who was now also a Flying Officer, having been promoted on 2 October 1943, was also there, as were some other members of the crew from their 76 Squadron days. Now they learnt the tactics and techniques of the Pathfinder Force.

The extra training required to become a Pathfinder was not in fact extensive. The use of flares of differing colours to mark both the way to the target and the target itself was simple enough to a crew who had seen them before. What had developed was even greater need for crew cooperation. With all the radio, navigation and bombing devices on a PFF Lancaster the three electronic operators – wireless operator, navigator, and bomb-aimer had to work as a team. Some flight engineers also trained as bomb-aimers. Jack and the rest of Hoover's crew had three days to practise, in mock operations on 2, 3 and 4 March. On 5 March 1944 they were posted to 35 Squadron. The squadron was based at RAF Graveley, about five miles from St Neots and seven miles from Huntingdon. The Commanding Officer of 35 Squadron was the much admired Wing Commander S. P. Daniels, the holder of two Distinguished Service Orders and two Distinguished Flying Crosses.

Chapter 10

The Third Tour – Pathfinder

If 1943 was the year in which it became possible to believe that the Allies could win the war, it was during 1944 that the key battles were won. The bomber offensive continued, but as time went by the need for effective cooperation between air, land and sea forces became more important. Whatever Harris may have thought of this derogation of Bomber Command's strategic role, the men and women under his command took the switch to tactical targets in their stride.

As we have seen, the effectiveness of Bomber Command had increased enormously since Jack's previous tour, through both experience and the application of new technology. Furthermore, the Americans had introduced long-range fighter aircraft to escort their daylight bombing formations. On 8 February 1944 a joint force of 350 American and British aircraft had attacked Frankfurt without loss, shooting down nineteen German fighters in the process. On the night of 15 February, the RAF had put 1,000 bombers over Berlin causing major disruption to communications. In other theatres, the Allies were advancing through Italy and, although Cassino was to hold them back, Mussolini was deposed. Meanwhile, in the Pacific the Japanese were being forced out of one island after another.

Jack's new squadron, No. 35, was first formed in the Royal Flying Corps on 1 February 1916, at Thetford, Norfolk. Towards the end of January 1917 the squadron went to France equipped with Armstrong Whitworth FK8s for army cooperation duties. The squadron had the distinction of having been specially trained for cooperation with the cavalry and it remained attached to the

Cavalry Corps throughout the First World War. It was disbanded in 1919 on its return to the UK.

The squadron re-formed as a bomber squadron in March 1929, initially flying de Havilland 9A biplanes, at Bircham Newton, Norfolk, the airfield where Jack crash-landed in December 1941. The DH9A had been a successful daylight bomber during the last months of the First World War, dropping bombs on German towns, but it was hardly a type fit even for the 1930s. They were soon replaced by Fairey IIIFs, a light day bomber which had much success in bush-wars in Africa but lacked the firepower and bomb payload necessary in a European conflict.

By 1932 the squadron had re-equipped again, this time with the Fairy Gordon, a more powerful version of the IIIF. In October 1935, 35 Squadron was deployed to the Middle East following the invasion of Abyssinia by the Italians. For ten months the squadron was based in the Sudan as a reinforcement to RAF Middle East Command. When it returned to UK it was based at Worthy Down during the latter part of 1937 where it exchanged its Gordons for Vickers Wellesleys. The Wellesley was an excellent aircraft for its day. A two-seat general purpose bomber with a 2,000lb bomb load and mounting one Vickers machine gun forward and one aft, its principle asset was its long range. In November 1938, it claimed the world longest flight record when two aircraft flew non-stop from Ismailia in Egypt to Darwin in Australia.

At the beginning of the Second World War, 35 Squadron became a training unit, briefly losing its squadron identity as No. 17 OTU. It was equipped with Bristol Blenheims, the first of the new monoplanes to be ordered under the RAF Expansion Scheme. However, in November 1940, the squadron was re-formed for the express purpose of introducing the new Handley Page Halifax into operational service. They flew their first sorties on the night of 11 March 1941, when the target was Le Havre. Six aircraft were dispatched, four of which successfully attacked the primary target whilst another, unable to see either the primary or the alternative target (Boulogne), bombed Dieppe instead. The sixth aircraft, failing to see the target even after repeated circuits and having insufficient fuel to allow it to proceed to the alternative, jettisoned its bombs in the Channel. Unfortunately, one of the aircraft which had bombed Le Havre was mistaken for an enemy aircraft on the return journey and was shot down in flames by RAF night fighters. Only two members of the crew – the pilot and the flight engineer – escaped by parachute and survived.

The squadron bombed a variety of targets in Germany and occupied France during 1941, some of the raids being undertaken in daylight. In July 1941 the squadron made its first raid on Berlin. Only two aircraft were detailed for the raid and the pilot of the only one to reach the target was Flying Officer Cheshire, who has already appeared in this story as the Officer Commanding 76 Squadron early in 1943. In September 1942 Cheshire made the 1,700-mile trip to Turin in Northern Italy. In February 1942, No. 38 was one of the squadrons which attempted to stop the German warships *Scharnhorst* and *Gneisenau* during their escape dash from Brest to North German ports. No. 35 Squadron continued to play a major part in historic Bomber Command raids, such as Le Creusot (19 June 1943), Peenemunde (17 August 1943) and many others. The squadron converted to Lancasters in March 1944, just before Jack joined it at RAF Gravely.

Graveley was a major bomber base constructed in 1941/42 to the west of Graveley village, about six miles south of Huntingdon and about the same distance north-east of St Neots. Most of its land was taken from Cotton Farm. Three runways were laid out, one of 1,600 yards and two of about 1,300 yards each. The usual pan-type hard standings were distributed round the perimeter track. There were four maintenance hangars. Flat-roofed administrative and accommodation buildings were to the north of the site. They were well apart from each other to minimise casualties should the *Luftwaffe* attempt a raid such as hit Linton-on-Ouse in May 1941, as described in Chapter 8. The accommodation was sufficient for 2,300 men and 300 women. Some of the personnel lived off camp, so the maximum strength of the base would be around 3,000.

The station briefly became operational in the spring of 1942 with the arrival of the Lysanders and Wellingtons of No. 161 Squadron, which was part of No. 3 Group. No. 161 Squadron was involved in special duties, including dropping and recovering secret agents working in enemy territory. They did not stay long at Graveley because the airfield was temporarily closed while its runways were lengthened, the main runway to 2,000 yards and the other two to 1,400 yards.

Following the extensions of the runways, Graveley was re-allocated to the Pathfinder Force of No. 8 Group in August 1942. The Headquarters of No. 8 Group was in Huntingdon, and Air Vice-Marshal Bennett wanted his squadrons close to his HQ. The nine airfields used by Pathfinder squadrons were: Graveley, Polebrook, Wyton, Bourn, Little Stoughton, Upwood, Gransden Lodge, Oakington, and Warboys. No. 35 Squadron was the first bomber squadron to arrive at Gravely, transferred from No. 4 Group at Linton-on-Ouse with its now more reliable Halifaxes. The first bombing operation from Graveley was on the night of 18 August 1942. A major development for No. 8 Group, covered elsewhere in this story, was the formation at Graveley, on New Year's Day 1944, of No. 692 Squadron with Mosquito aircraft. They flew their first sorties on 1 February 1944, becoming part of what was known as the Light Night Striking Force. In March, 35 Squadron exchanged its Halifaxes for Lancasters, which it operated until its final sorties on 25 April 1945. No. 692 Squadron's Mosquitos carried out their last raid on 3 May 1945 with an attack on Kiel. During its operational life, Graveley's squadrons lost eighty-three Halifaxes, thirty-two Lancasters and thirty-five Mosquitos; a total of 150 aircraft – an average of twelve each month.

In June 1945, 692 Squadron moved to Gransden Lodge and 227 Squadron, with Lancasters, joined 35 Squadron at Graveley to prepare for movement to the Far East as part of the 'Tiger Force', which was intended to join the USAAF in the strategic bombing offensive against Japan. The atomic bombs dropped on Hiroshima and Nagasaki made this unnecessary. No. 227 Squadron was disbanded in September and 115 Squadron moved into Graveley from Witchford to replace it. The Lancasters of 35 and 115 Squadrons remained at Graveley for another year before being transferred to Stradishall, which was a permanent camp. During this time, 35 Squadron took its Lancasters on a goodwill tour to the USA.

Graveley was put on care and maintenance in September 1945. No more RAF units were based there, but the hastily built wartime airfield was kept as a reserve for another twelve years. The main runway was maintained in good condition and was regularly used by training aircraft for 'circuits and bumps'. The airfield was finally closed at the end of 1968, its land being returned to Cotton Farm. The eastern end of the main runway still survived in the late 1990s, and part of the perimeter track is used by the farm. In 1944, however, the rural atmosphere shook with the noise of the RAF's most effective bomber types, the Lancaster and the Mosquito.

Without doubt, the Avro Lancaster was the outstanding RAF heavy bomber of the Second World War. Owen Thetford[1] illustrates this through a calculation of tons of bombs dropped for every aircraft lost. The four-engined heavies are the only candidates in the running, and the Lancaster easily leads the field:

Type	Tons dropped per aircraft lost
Lancaster	132
Halifax	56
Stirling	41

The Lancaster would probably not have been built if the twin-engined Avro Manchester had not been a disastrous failure. The Manchester had entered service in November 1941, and some took part in the Millennium raids in 1942, but the engines were prone to failure and the type was withdrawn from service at the end of June 1942.

Although rated as a two-engined bomber, the Manchester had the power of four engines and could thus carry the bomb load of a four-engined bomber. Rolls-Royce had paired two of their Kestrel engines to a common drive shaft and named the resulting engine the Vulture. Perhaps because of a mismatch of stress on its drive shaft the Vulture was prone to bearing failure, often leading to a fire in the engine – a severe hazard in any aircraft. The solution seems to have been identified early in 1940. Aircraft designers sometimes have to rely on inspiration. After a flight in the Manchester prototype, senior officers from the Air Staff in London were invited into the office of Avro's chief designer where, on a table, there was a model of the Manchester. Looking at the model, he asked his visitors if Rolls-Royce Merlin engines were now in full production, which in fact they were. He then showed how, by extending the wings of the Manchester, it would be possible to mount two Merlins on each wing to produce the same power as the Manchester obtained from its two Vultures. The result was the Lancaster, which first flew in January 1941.

With its four Roll-Royce Merlin engines, the Lancaster could achieve 287 mph at 11,500ft, and it had an operational range of 1,660 miles carrying 14,000 lb of bombs. It had a crew of seven: pilot, 2nd pilot/engineer, navigator, bomb-aimer, rear gunner, mid-upper gunner and wireless operator. Although initially designed to carry 4,000lb bombs, the Lancaster's bomb bay was able, in due course, to carry much heavier bombs. In April 1942, Lancasters dropped the first 8,000lb bomb on Essen. In September 1943 a 12,000lb bomb was dropped by 617 Squadron on the Dortmund-Ems canal. The 12,000lb 'Tallboy' bomb was first used against the Saumur tunnel on 8 June 1944, and the 'Grand Slam', weighing an amazing 22,000lb, was dropped for the first time on the Bielefeld viaduct in March 1945.

If required it was possible to fit a second control column and to operate with two pilots instead of one pilot and one flight engineer, but in Bomber Command's Lancasters, the flight engineer sat next to the pilot. The front gunner was positioned in front and a little below the pilot, and the other two were at the mid-upper and rear positions. The bomb-aiming position was in the usual position at the front looking down. The radio operator's cubicle was behind the pilot, close to the navigator's seat. It was fitted with the standard communications systems which Jack used in Pinocchio, his Halifax in 76 Squadron, but additional equipment was squeezed in. The most significant was the H2S ground-mapping radar display. The radar's rotating antenna was mounted in a radome beneath the aircraft, and its return energy was fed to a cathode ray tube only a few inches in diameter mounted in the bottom left hand corner of the wireless operator's desk. The H2S picture was used for both navigation and bomb-aiming: hence the need for close collaboration between crew members.

By 1945 the RAF had fifty-six Lancaster squadrons in the front line. The total production was 7,377, including 430 which were manufactured in Canada. Many modifications were made to the Lancaster for specific roles. The Merlin engines of the Mark III Lancaster as flown by 35 Squadron were made under licence in the USA by Packard. The last operational Lancaster was in the maritime reconnaissance role, from which it was retired in February 1954, only ten years after Jack was facing the hurdle of his third tour of duty in Bomber Command.

Neither the 35 Squadron nor the RAF Gravely Operations Record Books provide complete details of the crew of which Jack was a member. Hoover was, of course, the pilot and Jack was the wireless operator and later the bomb-aimer. The three other Canadians from the 76 Squadron tour were back home in Canada. Bill Lloyd and Cliff Hill made up the quartet remaining from of the previous tour. A new air gunner, Jock Mackenzie, became a regular crew member, but the navigator and bomb-aimer positions were not consistent through the tour. Cliff Hill moved to rear gunner, and Flight Sergeant Mackenzie took his place in the mid-upper turret. Based largely on Bill Lloyd's memory, the crew consisted of:

Flying Officer Harold Hoover pilot (now the only Canadian)

Flight Sergeant Bill Lloyd flight engineer

Flying Officer Phil (Shortie) Burt navigator until mid-May 1944

Flying Officer Geoff Goom bomb-aimer (until 12th July)

Flying Officer Jack Mossop w/op until early May, then bomb-aimer

Flight Sergeant Cliff Hill rear-gunner

Flight Sergeant Jock Mackenzie mid-upper gunner

Someone had decided that it would help bomber crews who were shot down if they carried photographs of themselves which the forgers of false identity papers in the resistance groups in occupied territory could use. In processing the photographs of

105

Hoover's crew someone made a mistake and made the prints too large. The wasted copies were given to the individuals concerned. Somehow the photographs of Jack Mossop, Jock Mackenzie, Cliff Hill and Hoover all ended in the possession of Jack. These four, plus Bill Lloyd, were the regular crew members. Phil Burt flew with them occasionally but he soon left to join another crew only to be shot down and killed over France sometime in May. Other navigators who flew with Jack on this tour were Flying Officer Roberts, who was also lost with another crew, and Warrant Officer Perkins. The bomb-aimer, Phil Goom left in July. The role of the bomb-aimer had changed by 1944, especially in Pathfinder squadrons. Indeed, many of the roles of a bomber crew were much less distinct. If the weather allowed visual sighting of the target, the flight engineer would often release the bombs, and the bomb-aimer would move back in the aircraft to help the navigator manipulate the H2S radar. In Hoover's crew, it seems that Jack left his radio kit to look after itself while he went to release the bombs.

As noted in Chapter 1, with very few exceptions, Jack only wrote in his diary for 1944 to record his observations on operations in which he flew. By linking his comments with the entries in both the 35 Squadron and the RAF Graveley ORBs we can build up a more complete record of this tour of operations than has been possible with the first two tours. However, for the first raid with his new squadron the diary entry is the only source, and it indicates a rather disappointing start:

Wednesday 22nd March 1944
(Op. 55)
Operations to Frankfurt. Not a success for us. Better luck next time. Quiet trip except for Flak over Lille on way back. Enjoyed trip, but Navigator 'boobed'. Whole raid fairly good – well concentrated.

Lacking a crew list for this operation we do not know who the navigator who 'boobed' was, nor do we know the consequences of the mistake. The squadron ORB records the loss of one crew. Altogether, twenty-two bombers were lost that night out of 816 detailed for the raid (2.7 per cent) – bad, but not nearly as bad as four days later when, on 26 March, 795 bombers attacked Nuremburg. Ninety-five bombers were lost; 12 per cent of the attacking force. It was Bomber Command's worst night of losses. Hoover's crew were lucky not to be detailed for that raid, but their raid, two days earlier on 24 March, was nearly as bad. They took part in the last of a series of raids on Berlin. In his excellent and highly detailed description of a Pathfinder squadron at war,[2] Michael Wadsworth uses this raid to demonstrate how the intricate planning required for strategic bomber operations can easily unravel. The plan sent 822 bombers on a route which took them out over the North Sea. With no land in sight for over two hours, the navigators had to rely on dead reckoning. However the wind was much stronger than forecast and the bomber stream was scattered. When the main force bombers reached the target, the target indicators had drifted off the aiming points, and only a few of the ground markers were visible through the cloud. Only aircraft fitted with H2S radar were able to find their way with any accuracy, and on the return leg many of the bombers were shot down by the flak batteries which surrounded other cities. Of 822 aircraft sent out, seventy-three (9 per cent) did not return. Loss rates around 10 per cent were not sustainable. Michael Wadsworth's father flew on this operation as flight engineer in a PFF Lancaster of 156 Squadron, and in his book he quotes from his father's log:

Coned over Ruhr for fifteen minutes. Aircraft hit by flak, and mid-upper gunner wounded. Very narrow escape.

Jack's diary entry supports Wadworth's description of the raid.

Friday 24th March 1944
(Op. 56)
Operations to Berlin. Whole raid pretty well flopped. We remained in T/Area for 40 mins – really tried. Bombed blindly – probably hit suburbs of Berlin. Just missed Munster defences on way home. Landed at Wyton.

There were seventy-five Pathfinders in this raid, and about 700 in the main force. Much later Cliff Hill produced a narrative of events. Hoover's crew flew out at a height 19,000 feet, as planned. However Geoff Goom, the bomb-aimer, soon found that the H2S radar display was showing the island of Sylt to port whilst the navigator, Phil Burt, believed it was to starboard. Jack obtained from Graveley the latest forecast wind speed, which was given as 80 knots, but Phil calculated that the wind must have been well over 100 knots. Hoover asked for a new course, while the remainder of the crew remained just a little concerned. Finally, Phil confirmed that they were over Denmark just north of Esbjerg. They skirted round neutral Sweden and crossed over the Baltic Sea. Hoover asked for a course to Berlin avoiding Rostock. Over to starboard there were signs of battle, with an aircraft coned by searchlights eventually catching fire and falling. Turning south, with the wind now behind them, they were on their last leg to the target. They could see aerial combats with fighters circling above the bomber stream. They arrived over the target two minutes early with nothing happening, so Hoover flew a half circle to line up with the bomber stream. Their task on the raid was to act as a supporter, dropping markers to show the way when approaching the target, and dropping bombs when they reached the target. When they ran in to bomb, the target indicators from earlier Pathfinder bombers had drifted on the strong wind. With eight-tenths cloud cover little could be seen of the ground, and it was difficult to achieve the concentration of bomb hits which was needed to cause the desired effect of devastation of part of the city. Hoover decided to go round again. The cloud tops were at 5,000 feet, making the earlier markers difficult to see, but Geoff Goom bombed on a conflagration which was big enough to illuminate the cloud base. They flew home south of Hanover, keeping clear of the Ruhr Valley, where the defences around Essen, Duisberg and Dortmund would be too hazardous, although Jack's diary entry indicates that they were a bit too far north as they nearly ran into the defences around Munster. Their H2S radar had developed a fault just before they had reached Berlin and was of no use in helping the navigator on the return journey.

There is no indication of why they landed at Wyton. It is only six miles from Graveley, and the most likely reason is that runway congestion necessitated a diversion. They landed at 3.20 a.m. after a round trip of 7½ hours. RAF transport took them to

Graveley for debriefing, and they could have slept until around mid-day. By 4.00 p.m. next day they were all back at Wyton to fly the Lancaster to Graveley, taking the opportunity to practise blind approach procedures using the new radio landing aids. The next day they had a cross-country exercise starting at 11.00 a.m. and the day after they were over Essen, with some slightly more encouraging results, despite continuing concern over navigation.

Sunday 26th March 1944
(Op. 57)
Operations to Essen. Pretty good raid, tho' target obscured by cloud. Nav not so good again – Nav 2 very good. Bill said bombs gone before B/doors open. Lots of fighters. Flak not up to usual Essen standard.

Trying to release the bombs before opening the bomb doors would have no effect. The bomb release system in a Lancaster would only work after the doors began to open, but bombs could be released before the doors were fully open. The reason for this slightly odd logic is that crews may have to jettison bombs in circumstances where the bomb doors were jammed partially open. Because the opening of bomb doors has an impact on aircraft handling, the bomb door control was mounted on the left hand side of the cockpit, where only the pilot could reach it.[3] Bill Lloyd admitted to me that he was a little early when he said 'bombs gone'. He was prone in the bomb-aimer's position at the time, as Geoff Goom, the designated bomb-aimer was in the navigator's position using the H2S radar on the run-in to the target. Hoover immediately opened the bomb doors on Bill's call. As Bill put it, there was a bit of clanging from the bomb bay, but all the bombs dropped with no harm to the aircraft. They still seemingly lacked a regular navigator. 'Nav 2' was probably an un-crewed navigator, drafted in to help in managing the new electronic systems. Pathfinder Lancasters often flew with eight in the crew, but this was the only such occasion in Hoover's crew.

After the Berlin raid on 24 March, Hoover's crew were allocated their own aircraft, 'O' Oscar and they used it during the next two weeks eight times on non-operational cross-country exercises with no operational trip. They also had a fighter affiliation exercise. It may of course be a coincidence, but perhaps the Commanding Officer had told them to sharpen up in anticipation of daylight tactical operations ahead. Jack made two significant entries in his diary during this period. On 29 March he wrote:

Don't forget Hilda's birthday 8th April.

And, on 8 April, in case he might have forgotten, with an asterisk for emphasis and a circle round the figure 8 he wrote:

Hilda's birthday.

The date is correct. She may or may not have been twenty-one years old. Hilda's age was, and remains, a state secret. War is no respecter of birthdays, however. On the day itself, Jack was airborne for 3 hours and 50 minutes on a cross-country naviga-tion exercise. Jack and Hilda had known each other for just over one year, meeting about once a month. If he missed her coming of age party, he was soon to make amends.

In addition to the daylight training flights, Jack also had three sessions in a Link Trainer. The Link was an early and, by today's standards, a rather crude flight simulator. Its main purpose was to provide practice in the art of keeping an aircraft in flight. The balance between roll, pitch, and yaw, the three axes of movement of an aircraft in controlled flight, is central to a pilot's skill. Jack had two sessions in a Link Trainer for familiarisation training on 5 and 6 April, and a third on 16 April logged as 'Turns – "T" Test'. It is not clear why Jack did this training. It may have been at his own initiative, simply to understand more about the pilot's job. However, it could also have been an official requirement to provide a last-ditch means of controlling an aircraft if both the pilot and flight engineer were incapacitated. With such minimal training the best that could be expected would be to hold the stricken aircraft sufficiently under control while the crew bailed out.

Wednesday 11th April
  (Op. 58)
  Operations to Aachen. A quiet trip. Dropped 12 1-thousand pounders on target. Little flak, no searchlights. Enjoyed trip except for 40 mins wait in circuit for landing.

There is nothing new about air traffic delays, but any frustration would have been ameliorated by the prospect of a period without operations. On 13 and 15 April, the crew again flew on cross-country daylight training exercises, including air to surface firing of their guns. Jack's next diary entry is not until 26 April, but it was very significant:

Last day of a wonderful leave

Hilda and Jack had married on Wednesday 19 April 1944 at Medomsley Church, near Consett, in County Durham. They had a seven-day honeymoon in Edinburgh, one consequence of which was that their only child, Bill, was born on 22 January 1945, precisely nine months and three days after the wedding. My mother once apologised to me for those three days, as if she had wasted them. There was one anxious moment during the honeymoon. A telegram arrived at their hotel from the Commanding Officer of 35 Squadron, Wing Commander Daniels, causing an immediate concern that Jack was recalled from leave. In fact it carried congratulations on Jack's promotion to Acting Flight Lieutenant, which would become effective on 26 May. They returned from Edinburgh on 26 April, a Wednesday. Hilda stayed the night with her new parents-in-law in Durham. She had unknowingly pleased her mother-in-law by giving me the second name of Wayne. Her mother-in-law's maiden name had been Waine: different spelling and an accidental compliment, but well received. Jack meanwhile had to report for duty. He may have taken a night train to St Neots, the nearest railway station to Graveley. As a commissioned officer he would have been required to travel first class, but his next diary entry suggests that he had little rest, possibly because he reverted to hitch-hiking, which was his habitual mode of transport.

27th April 1944
(Op. 59)
Travelled back from leave overnight – no sleep – and on ops tonight. Target Freidrichshafen. Managed to stay awake throughout an excellent trip. Whole raid seemed to be a great success. Have every reason to believe we were 'bang on

Aiming Point'. Only snag – 50 miles off-track on French coast coming back.

This was another long trip. They were airborne for 6 hours and 50 minutes. Still, despite being off-track on the homeward leg, Jack seems quite pleased with the results; not to mention being able to stay awake. The nature of the bombing campaign produced some strange ironies, unique to air warriors. There was no other group of combatants who could be enjoying a week's leave in the relative safety and comfort of Edinburgh, a week which on this occasion served as a honeymoon, yet within a few hours of returning to duty find themselves airborne en route to bomb an enemy city, facing the combined risk associated with collisions, engine failure, enemy night fighters and flak, both en route and over the target area. It is not at all strange that Jack told his new wife very little about his job.

Jack's satisfaction over the night's work at Freidrichshafen on 27 April was shared by others. Wing Commander Max Hunt, a New Zealander then commanding 75 (NZ) Squadron, confirms there was bright moonlight over the target and that the bombing accuracy was almost perfect.[4] The target was a factory making tank engines and gearboxes. An anonymous contributor to the 35 Squadron ORB recorded:

Target identified on H2S and by red and green target indicators. The first white flares went out at 0200 hours. Red and green target indicators were seen a few minutes later. Although lots of reds were down at time of bombing, two quite close together and one some distance away, aircraft bombed the centre one, raid appeared well concentrated but position of target indicators on target could not be seen.

The next trip went well too:

Sunday 30th April 1944
  (Op. 60)
  Operations to Achères near Paris (marshalling yards). Short and quiet trip. Definitely hit target. One bomb hung-up. ('Pongo'.)

A 'Pongo' is an operation in support of the Army. This is the first indication of 35 Squadron being diverted from strategic targets to pave the way for the Normandy invasion. Jack calls it a short trip, but it still required 3 hours and 45 minutes flying time, taking off at 10.22 p.m. There were to be many more Pongos, both in the weeks before D-Day and after the landings.

Operations over France had been seen as relatively safe, to the extent that they counted only as one third of an operation when it came to completing a full tour of thirty, or a total of ninety operations. However, Jack was lucky in this regard. The policy was changed with effect 1 May 1944, when it became clear that the enemy's air defences over northern France had been strengthened in anticipation of an invasion. The Achères raid on 30 April 1944 was Jack's only operation over northern France before the change in the rule. His final tally of operations was thus eighty-nine and one third, rounded up to ninety.

Wednesday 3rd May 1944
(Op. 61)
Another 'Pongo' – to aerodrome at Mont Didier, France. Did the bomb-aiming myself. Lovely trip – saw everything perfectly. All bombs on Target. After bombing had slight combat with JU88.

This entry is of interest for two reasons. First, it is one of only two occasions, during the 1944 tour at least, that Jack was involved in air-to-air conflict. The Junkers 88 was a long range fighter which had caused many casualties in Coastal Command during operations over the Atlantic. Second, Jack acted as bomb-aimer. In all his previous operational sorties he was rated as the wireless operator, and he would man the guns if needed. However, the new technology installed in the Lancaster required some flexibility of labour. The H2S equipment was primarily a navigation aid, so it was used by the navigator for most of the time. When over the target area however, H2S became a bomb-aiming tool. Bomb-aimers were also therefore trained in its use. While he was manipulating H2S, the bomb-aimer could not also release the weapons onto the target. As indicated in Chapter 9, the new technology had removed much of the distinction of roles

113

in a heavy bomber. Jack and Geoff Goom had become system operators along with the various navigators in the crew during this tour. In this and subsequent operations, he is rated in his log book as 'bomb-aimer (v)' – the 'v' indicating volunteer. He was not the only one in the crew to take up what we would now call a wider skill set; Bill Lloyd often found himself in the bomber-aimer's station.

An entry in the RAF Graveley ORB for this raid, which did not include Hoover's crew, illustrates the extent of the tactical control vested in the master bomber at this stage of the campaign:

> Target visually on runways; red spot line, green target indicator seen in bomb sight. On approach saw red spot marker on ground West of N/S runway. Master Bomber instructed not to bomb. Orbited awaiting instructions. Two green TIs followed – one was approx a mile to S/W of red spot. Second green TI was near hangar and close to yellow TI. MB instructed to bomb on green TI near hangar. Concentration appeared well concentrated near target indicators, causing smoke and dust.

The sortie planned on 6 May did not start until 00.45 on 7 May:

> Saturday 6th May 1944
>   (Op. 62)
>   'Pongo' to marshalling yard at Mantes-Gassicourt, near Paris. Perfect visibility. Bombs right on Aiming Point. A short and pleasant trip. New Nav did very well. Did bomb-aiming myself.

The flying time was only three hours. Jack seems, at last, to have a navigator he could trust. The few comments in his diary critical of crew members all relate to navigational errors, which may be a little unfair given the difficulties which all Bomber Command squadrons had with navigation throughout the bombing campaign. Despite that, a sense of satisfaction now begins to emerge from the diary entries. This could be because with smaller, more precise, targets it was easier to assess the impact of the raid. An individual crew would have little idea how much they had contributed to a successful raid on a big city, whereas the tactical bombing primarily of well-defined military targets allowed an immediate assessment of the value each bomber made to the operation. But the sense of satisfaction could also result from a feeling that the task was now under control. No longer did they fly blindly over enemy territory hoping to find the target, and when they had found it no longer did they see from the automatic photographs that only a few bombs actually struck home. It would, of course, never be easy, as the next two extracts show.

The entry in the RAF Graveley ORB relating to the 6 May raid provides a good indication of the role, and the frustrations, of the master bomber as a tactical airborne commander:

> The Master Bomber clearly identified the A/P and attempted to mark it with TI Yellow at 0209.30 but the markers fell too far to the west so he instructed the main force to ignore them. TIs then fell slightly to the south of A/P followed by a Yellow to the north of it. MB instructed a/c to bomb these, but the instruction was made confusing by further TIs falling nearby. The Deputy MB was therefore instructed to mark the A/P with white TIs . This was done by 0216 but by that time smoke had obscured the yards, and Main Force were then instructed to bomb the centre of the fires which appeared to be centred on very near the A/P. All ac bombed on instruction form the MB, and though the raid appeared to be successful, most crews felt that confusion was caused by too many flares and TIs.

And, from Jack's diary, four days later:

> Wednesday 10th May 1944
> (Op. 63)
> Operation ('Pongo') to Lens in France. Bombed marshalling yards. Results not so good – we only just hit edge of target. A very quiet and short trip.

Although originally a volunteer for the role, Jack was now the designated bomb-aimer in the crew. Since 2 May, in addition to operational flying, he had been airborne on four daylight practice sorties which included bombing practice. The Lens raid had lasted 2 hours 15 minutes, landing back at base thirty-five minutes after midnight. The crew's debriefing report appears in the 35 Squadron ORB:

As we ran towards target the MB instructed to hold off for 3 mins. Did an oval orbit and came back to bomb white T/I, seen in bomb sight. Just after bombing, the area became covered with smoke but a quick visual of yard showed the TI white to be at NW end of SE section of the yard.

The following day's operation was better:

Thursday 11 May 1944
(Op. 64)
Operation ('Pongo') to Louvain in Belgium. Pretty good show. A quiet trip for us but we saw two a/c go down in flames.

However, not everyone thought it a pretty good show. An entry in the RAF Graveley ORB reads:

The MB was clearly heard, but it was thought that too few instructions were given to the Main Force.

The ORBs were classified documents, and it was acceptable to record what might be thought of as critical comments of a senior officer. Not that the master bomber was necessarily a senior officer; they were chosen on experience and knowledge as well as rank. There then followed a seven day gap in operational flying which was given over to intensive training, including cross-country exercises, air-to-sea firing, bombing practice and fighter affiliation. There seems little doubt that these exercises were directly related to the forthcoming Normandy landings. Everybody had to be ready for the invasion.

Then it was back to the dangerous work: take-off 23.59, for a short operation, flying time 2 hours 45 minutes:

Friday 19 May 1944
(Op. 65)
Operation – marshalling yards at Boulogne – a short excellent trip. Made three runs over Target. Got bombs away

116

on third run. Right on Aiming Point. Excellent photo'.

As already noted, the photographs brought back were vital evidence of the competence of the crew. When Jack writes 'excellent photo' in his diary, he is referring to the quality of the bombing rather than of the photograph itself.

Despite the demands of the invasion planners, the strategy of keeping a round-the-clock bombing campaign against German industry capability required the bomber squadrons to switch from the tactical to the strategic role with no more than a day's notice. This flexibility which relies, of course, on intensive training and high skill levels, is a significant feature of air power.

> Sunday 21 May 1944
>   (Op. 66)
>   Operations – back to Germany with a raid on Duisburg (Ruhr). Whole raid a flop – 10/10 cloud over Target. Markers didn't turn up. We intended to bomb on T but had bomb door trouble so we overshot and bombed Krefeld. What might be called an abortive sortie!

Jack is being a little hard on himself and his crew. Once the bomb door problem was fixed they would have been justified in simply jettisoning the bombs to improve manoeuvrability should they encounter a German night fighter. The RAF Graveley ORB tells us:

> Aircraft C bombed Krefeld as a last resort target as his bombs failed to release over the primary.

The crew's report as recorded in the 35 Squadron ORB sheds a bit more light on the matter:

> On run up over primary, no lights on bomb door circuit or in bomb door panel. Having a good H2S picture of Krefeld on homeward run attempted again with success.

There is an almost nostalgic air to the next diary entry:

> Monday 22 May 1944
>   (Op. 67)
>   Operation to Dortmund. An excellent trip. No trouble at

all. The Valley looked its old self – hundreds of searchlights and heavy Flak. Saw a few a/c go down in flames.

The valley was, of course, the Ruhr and this was Jack's last operation to it. Dortmund is not very far away, just over 4 hours there and back, but it had comprehensive defences. Aachen, where they went two days later (24 May), is about the same distance, but the round trip took 40 minutes less, probably because of selective routeing to avoid air and ground defences. There is no sense of nostalgia this time.

Wednesday 24th May 1944
(Op. 68)
Operation to Aachen. A short trip. Two minutes late in bombing but right on the point. Had no trouble but saw a lot of fighters. Saw a/c shot down into sea.

Both ORBs are blank for seven days at this point, so Jack's diary and log book are the only sources, although his service record does at least provide evidence of his promotion to the rank of Acting Flight Lieutenant, with effect from 26 May 1944. The pendulum now swings, and the squadron is back in a tactical role, softening logistics targets in northern France.

Saturday 27 May 1944
(Op. 69)
Operations – military camp and depot at Bourg-Leopold in Belgium. Dropped white markers on A/P. Also a 'cookie'. A good target well-pranged. (Hilda staying near the camp for the week-end. Hope she wasn't worrying tonight).

A 'cookie' was a 4,000 pound bomb – nearly two tons. This diary entry, for 27 May, is the only one which mixes duty with pleasure – or at least with anticipated pleasure.

They landed on Sunday morning, 28 May, at about 04.00. Hilda had travelled down from Newcastle the previous day and was staying in an hotel in St Neots. She had wanted to stay up until Jack could join her, but the hotelier pointed out that the aircrew who had been in the bar earlier in the day had all been drinking lemonade, suggesting that they were due to fly that night, so she retired alone. Jack made it to her bedroom at about 4.00 a.m. local time. They had a few days and hours of peace. Hilda was two months pregnant. Whit Monday was on 29 May, not that it had any influence on the flying programme, but Jack had a day off work. They spent their time together walking round the lanes of Huntingdonshire. Jack was required for a bombing and map reading exercise on 30 May, and Hilda returned home to Medomsley on 31 May, a day on which Jack had fighter affiliation, bombing, and air-to-sea firing exercises in the morning, prior to a briefing for a midnight operation due to take off at 22.55.

Wednesday 31st May 1944
(Op. 70)
Shortest possible trip to Military HQ and radar jammer at Mont Couple near Calais. Excellent bombing. Got a picture of the Aiming Point. Airborne 1 hour 40 minutes only. Excellent photo.

RAF Graveley's ORB is a somewhat more reticent about claiming success:

Radar jammer – precision attack. The MB's instructions were heard by only one ac which bombed slightly S/W of green TIs, which MB stated was the 100 yards East of A/P.

Despite Jack's delight in the excellence of the bombing, this raid was, in fact, a failure. Professor R.V. Jones tells the story in *Most Secret War*.[5] The D-Day invasion fleet would rely on the GEE navigational system, but it was known that the Germans could interfere with the GEE signals using jamming transmitters. There were five of these jammers in northern France, one of which was at Mont Couple, near Boulogne. Reconnaissance photographs taken the day after the raid showed that the bombs had been concentrated in a small field to one side of the jamming site. The bombing was spectacularly accurate, but the target marker had been 100 yards off the aiming point, and only one bomber heard the MB's instruction to correct the error. Presumably the MB's radio transmitter was faulty. Bomber Command was asked to launch another raid which took place two days later, this time successfully, but Jack was busy elsewhere that night. Professor Jones records that all five jammer sites were destroyed by bombing before D-Day. Jack continued in his efforts to disrupt the French railway system around Paris.

Friday 2nd June
(Op. 71)
Another marshalling Yard – at Trappes, a few miles S.W. of Paris. Dropped White T.I.s,[6] a cookie, and 2x1,000 lb right on yard. A nice trip for us, though attacked by a fighter. Saw about 12 a/c go down in flames. Very good photo.

Trappes is a little more than 'a few' miles from Paris, more like thirty miles. The 35 Squadron ORB has this to say:

Clouds of smoke and fire toward end and master bomber instructed later arrivals to bomb centre of conflagration and smoke.

Events were now moving fast. Jack's diary entry for 5 June 1944 is longer than usual:

Monday 5 June 1944
(Op. 72)
Night of 5-6 June. It became rather obvious during the day and at ops briefing that this was IT. We were to bomb coastal batteries at Maisy on French coast. A late take-off at 0135. On the way out saw Gliders Towed and Troop carrying a/c formatting. We bombed precisely on A/P, also marked it, and saw 'invasion fleet' on way back. A quiet trip for us but the beginning of great things.

The last six words of the diary entry are underlined – a rare emphasis in the diary. They had flown over the D-Day invasion fleet at about 3.00 a.m. The target for 35 Squadron was enemy gun emplacements at Maisy, on the mouth of the River Vire, between what were soon to be known as Utah and Omaha beaches. The squadron ORB carries a report from another crew:

Identified target visually and by fork in main road and wood in the fork. TI red seen to fall North West of target and about

120

4 TIs to East and South East. Centre of target indicators red and green seen in bombsight. One red seen about 1200 yards East of target which attracted some bombing. Majority of bombing was seen around one target indicator green in later stages.

One small detail is missing from these accounts of an historic event: by coincidence, Harold Hoover was promoted to flight lieutenant with effect 6 June 1944. His promotion made no difference to crew relationships; the pilot was always the skipper.

The next raid was to bomb enemy gun emplacements at St Lô; a night operation taking off at 2310 on 6 June 1944. It marks an interesting phase in Jack Mossop' s development. To take the evidence piece by piece, the RAF Graveley ORB records:

Two Lancasters of 35 Squadron took off from Graveley to act as MB and DMB in an attack on St Lo in co-operation with 5 Mosquitoes of PFF and heavies of 4 Group.

The 35 Squadron ORB contains the debriefing reports of the MB and the DMB, and identifies the MB as the Officer Commanding 35 Squadron, Wing Commander Daniels:

MB: Pilot: Wing Commander Daniels (OC 35 Squadron): DMB dropped white at 01.30 hours; fell approx 500 yards overshoot. Main Force instructed to bomb starboard red target indicator. Bombing concentration appeared reasonable.
   DMB: Target identified by red target indicators and visually. Approx 10 mins before ETA, broke cloud and ran up at 5500 feet. Saw red TI in bombsight on approach – bombed same. Several fires seen burning in town.

The phrase 'saw red TI in bomb site' suggests that Jack Mossop submitted the report himself. Finally, Jack's diary entry shows that Hoover's crew had been detailed as deputy master bomber (DMB), for the first time:

Tuesday 6 June 1944
   (Op. 73)
   Deputy Master Bomber on an important road centre town

through which Jerry reserves were coming. St Lo in Normandy. Cloudy all day and over Δ – we bombed rather low level. Our marker close to A/P and bombs 'bang on'. Good photograph.

It was Jack's accuracy in laying the marker flare which was the significant contribution to the success of the raid. In some ways, despite the shorter distance to the target and the less demanding navigation, the master bomber role was actually more hazardous in these tactical operations, because of the need to remain at low level over the target for a considerable period of time. Two nights later, Jack was again in the DMB aircraft attacking another tactical target:

Thursday 8 June 1944
  (Op. 74)
  DMB again at another communications centre at Mayenne, south of the battle front. Weather was awful – thick cloud and rain all the way but, amazingly, it was clear over the target. Right on the A/P with markers and bombs and got another good photo! On way back saw activity on 'Second Front'. Dreadful landing conditions – cloud down to 100 ft and heavy rain. Was complimented by C.O. for recent raids.

That compliment, based on his CO's personal observation on 6 June as well as the crew's debriefing reports after each raid, may have been simply an indication that another medal was in the offing, but it was probably more than that. Evidence from his own diary and from the records in the two ORBs suggests that, at the age of twenty-four years, Jack had become a highly proficient aviator, able to manage all the new technology by then available to the Lancaster crews of the Pathfinder Force. He was never one to show emotion, but he was a natural leader; someone whom others would trust. He could be forceful when appropriate, but since his views were reinforced by ability he was always likely to win an argument.

He was, however, due some leave. His diary, sparse as ever on issues not directly relevant to operational flying, simply records 'on leave' on 10 June, and 'back from leave' on 23 June. He spent his leave in Co Durham; he and Hilda staying with his parents in Durham City and her parents at Medomsley. The rule was still that one week's leave should be taken every six weeks during an operational tour.

When he returned from leave he was to find that a new type of target had appeared. The Germans had begun a bombardment of London using flying bombs, the V1 vengeance weapon. The V1 was a strategic weapon which had no tactical value. It was a flying bomb which killed and maimed, but its destruction was random. Its single purpose was to terrorise the population of targeted cities and thus to undermine the confidence and authority of their leaders. London was particularly vulnerable because the coastlines of France, Belgium and Holland formed a long arc which was in V1 range of central London. The bombs fell out of the sky when their fuel ran out, with a tendency to fall short rather than long. Both fighter aircraft and anti-aircraft guns could shoot them down, but by the time they were detected by ground radar they were already over the English coastline. Furthermore, shooting them down only resulted in a hit on a part of London other than where the bomb would have fallen anyway. The immediate British response to the threat was to move the many hundreds of anti-aircraft guns installed in north and central London to the coast east and south of the capital. This was done in quick order and in due course the V1 threat diminished, but meanwhile it was necessary to convince the population that direct action was being taken by the government and the military;[7] hence Jack's next target. The UK code-word for the V1 was P-Plane, as used in his diary record:

Saturday 24th June 1944
  (Op. 75)
  Operations – bombing P Plane launching sites at Rimeux in Pas de Calais. Pretty good trip, a lot of S'Lights strangely enough.

No. 35 Squadron's ORB reveals that only two of their aircraft were detailed for this raid in cooperation with five Pathfinder Mosquitos and 100 Lancasters of 3 Group.

Despite the bombing of launch sites, the Germans were capable of launching 200 V1s a day. Jack wrote in his diary:

Tuesday 27th June 1944
(Op. 76)

P Plane site again at Biennais in France. As we went out saw some of the P Planes on way to London. Cloudy over Target so retained T.I.s but bombed through cloud. Trip otherwise OK. Very quiet.

The RAF Graveley ORB suggests that Biennais was not a launch site, rather a storage depot:

Supply Site (P-Plane site). Two Lancasters of 35 Squadron were detailed to attack Rimeux in cooperation with 5 Mosquitos of PFF and 100 Lancasters of 3 Group (same force as previous raid).

Pathfinder Mosquitos used Oboe equipment to mark the target, but cloud may have hidden their markers so Jack and the other Pathfinder Lancasters used their H2S radars to lay down more markers. The third attack on V1 launch sites was in daylight.

Friday 30th June 1944
(Op. 77)

Daylight raid on P Planes at Oisement (France). Cloud over Target – dropped bombs only. Had fighter escort but did not need them. Small amount of heavy Flak. Very impressive sight seeing so many a/c bombing in daylight.

Heavy bomber crews would rarely see each other once airborne because they usually flew at night. Jack's few daylight raids were generally small affairs. The crew was DMB for this raid. However, it is obvious from the Graveley ORB that this raid was unlikely to have been successful:

Weather 10/10 cloud. Both ac withheld their TI's and bombed on GEE DR. No Mosquito TIs being seen and no visual pinpoints obtained before bombing. At least half the Main Force dropped before H-hour and the bombing appeared scattered.

It is not clear how effective these raids were. Professor R.V. Jones points out that the Germans could quickly erect and dismantle the

124

ramps from which the flying bombs were launched.[8] Using heavy bombers to counter such a nimble threat would not have been a good use of a valuable resource. From early July, the bombers were targeted on V1 supply depots rather than the launch sites. Jack's crew was tasked to bomb V1 sites four more times, but the priority was now turning to ensure that the Allied armies, landed in Normandy, could break out from the beach heads.

Tuesday 4th July
  (Op. 78)
  Marshalling Yd at Villeneuve-St-Georges nr Paris. Did three runs on Target dropping Illumins and 8 1,000lb bombs. Markers (red) were off but we hit Δ. Saw 6 a/c shot down by fighters on way back. We used cloud cover. (After take-off saw 4th July celebrations.)

The RAF Graveley ORB records that two of the aircraft shot down were from 35 Squadron. Jack uses the Greek delta letter (Δ) when referring to the target. It is a navigator's symbol, often called a cocked hat, formed when the direction of radio beacons or visual sightings are plotted on chart. The bearings of three beacons or visual sightings form the three sides of the Δ. The navigator's position or, as in this case, the target is somewhere inside the triangle. Jack is obviously delighted that they hit the target with their bombs, having previously dropped illuminator flares on probably two runs to the target before dropping bombs on a third run. There is an air of satisfaction about hitting the target despite the marker flares being off the target. There is, however, no sense of bragging or 'shooting a line' in RAF parlance. These words were written in a diary which no one knew about until long after the war was over. It is not clear where the 4 July celebrations were taking place, but there were several American squadrons at airfields in the Huntingdon area.

Jack's fourth raid on a V1 launch site, and the second in daylight, came next.

Thursday 6 July 1944
  (Op. 79)
  Daylight on P-Planes site at Marquise nr Calais. (Master Bomber). Perfectly clear weather. Bombed visually on A/P.

Saw bombs straddle A/P. Did another run to drop markers and stayed in the Δ area throughout raid b'casting bombing instructions. Fair amount of heavy flak.

Marquise is a village half way between Calais and Boulogne. As with all the operations since early May, Jack was the bomb-aimer on this raid. But on this raid, the crew was designated master bomber for the first time. So the whole raid depended on Jack getting his initial marker flares in the right place with absolute accuracy. They then stayed over the target to instruct the remaining bomber crews where to put their bombs. Jack kept a copy of the photograph, timed at 0819.12 sec, taken from his aircraft during this raid. The smoke surrounding the target area is impressive evidence of concentrated bombing, but nonetheless there are many bomb craters some way off the target.

The RAF Graveley ORB records that on 6 July 1944:

Two Lancasters took off from Graveley to act as MB and DMB in an attack on Marquise in co-operation with 5 Mosquitoes of PFF and 100 heavies of 4 Group. The weather was clear with good visibility. The red TIs went down on time and were backed up by TI yellows from the Master and Deputy Master Bombers. The Main Force acted on instruction received from the Master Bomber which resulted in good concentration of bombing.

The 35 Squadron ORB also records details of the squadron's involvement, in a debriefing report from Jack's crew as master bomber:

MB. At 0819.30, instructed Main Force to bomb between two puffs of smoke from target indicators. Aircraft orbited & dropped yellow target indicators which fell slightly East of aiming point – seen in bombsight. Main Force instructed to bomb slightly to starboard of yellow target indicators and in middle of smoke at 0824 hours. Bombing was well concentrated on aiming point although there were one or two undershoots, and one stick very close to tunnel entrance to NE of aiming point.

While 35 Squadron had been diverted by the V1 threat to London, the Allies were having difficulty in breaking out from Normandy, and now the priority was direct support to the Allied armies. Jack's diary gives the details:

Friday 7th July 1944
(Op. 80)
Daylight (evening) on military Target at Caen (helping out the Army). Extremely well concentrated raid – right on the A/P. Saw two a/c shot down by flak. C in C beach-head sent a telegram of thanks. Our markers recentred the concentration late on in the attack.

It was the task of Pathfinder squadrons to re-mark the target as a raid progressed. The first set of marker flares might have been obscured by smoke, or made less precise because of wind, or there could be tactical reasons for moving the concentration of the bombing to a different part of the target. Anyone in the target area that evening must have felt the impact of a disciplined and controlled bombing force. The British Commander-in-Chief, who was Field Marshal Montgomery, was certainly impressed. As recorded in the RAF Graveley ORB, his telegraphic message read:

Heavy bomber attack just taken place. A wonderfully impressive show and was enormously appreciated by the Army. The Army would like their appreciation and thanks sent to all crews.

The Station ORB also noted:

Explosions were continuous and some were very impressive.

Montgomery's message was well received by the squadron, and it was one of only a few times when Jack was moved to tell Hilda a little of what he did. It would seem from these records that the bombers had been effective in opening up a channel through which the Allied ground forces could advance. However, in his book *D-Day Bombers: The Veterans' Story*,[9] Stephen Darlow notes that when British soldiers advanced the next day, confident that the bombardment would have greatly weakened the enemy, they encountered unexpectedly stubborn resistance. Darlow also quotes from records held in the National Archives of post-war interrogations of German commanders. Colonel Kurt Meyer, commanding 12th Panzer Division, stated:

> As a result of the allied attack on Caen, the Div again endured heavy losses, 25 SS PGR being the chief sufferer, the first bn (battalion) having only 200 men left, the second bn a like number and the third bn hardly 100. The losses were caused not by the allied bomber attacks, but mainly by flame throwers that attacked immediately the bombing ceased, and as a result, caught the men in a somewhat dazed condition. It was only the arrival of 21 Panzer that saved what might have been a very ugly situation.

It had been a very large raid. Darlow points to 467 RAF bombers and 2,276 tons of high explosive bombs, most of them fused with a six-hour delay. Jack released his bombs early in the raid at about 9.30 p.m., but the main force bombers were still in the area after midnight. Add six hours for the time delay on the fuses to activate, and the bombs would be exploding between 0330 and 0600, a very discordant dawn chorus waiting for Colonel Meyer's surviving soldiers to emerge from their bunkers or shell holes; easy targets for the British flame-throwers. British and Canadian divisions made gains over the next few days, but this was still not the breakthrough that some had expected.

Two days later, however, 35 Squadron was again dealing with the V1 threat.

Sunday 9th July 1944
(Op. 81)
Master Bomber on daylight ops. P Plane site at Les Catelliers. In cloud all way to enemy coast. About 5/10 cloud over Δ. Red marker off, but we marked within 100yds of A/P. Lot of scattered bombing by M/F (Main Force) and consider raid to have been half-successful but you never can tell. Cloud prevented good observation of bombing and, it being such a small A/P, it could have been wiped out.

The voice of an experienced professional is now emerging, confident in understanding the options, expert in judging the shots, and realistic in estimating the success of the raid. RAF crew always work as a team, but Jack seems now to have emerged as the natural leader. Being the master bomber for the raid is simply a statement of fact.

The 35 Squadron ORB provides good detail on this raid:

> MB: Wing Commander Daniels; ac 'C': arrived on target at 13.29 hours. On arrival no bombing had taken place. Broadcast to Main Force 'basement clear'. At 1330 hours Main Force instructed to bomb to starboard, i.e. SW, of red target indicator. Instructions continually broadcast until DMB's yellow TIs fell at 1332 approx 200 yards South of Aiming Point. Main Force then instructed to bomb 200 yards to port of yellow, own TI yellow dropped at 1336 fell 100 yards SSW of aiming point on edge of wood. Main Force still instructed to bomb to port 100 yards, within 1,600 yards. Left target area at 1340 hours. Some scattered bombing still taking place.
>
> DMB: Master Bomber's instructions received clearly. Bombing appeared scattered despite MB's endeavours to check.

The Station ORB record is compatible with the squadron version, but much shorter:

> The target was successfully marked and the marking was corrected by directions given by the MB. Several sticks of bombs straddled the A/P but bombing generally was rather (illegible).

Hoover's crew had been allocated aircraft tail letter C for this and the previous operation The squadron ORB is clear that the squadron commander, Wing Commander Daniels, was the pilot of aircraft tail letter C, but it is not clear whether Daniels flew as first pilot or as 'second dicky'. In his Flying Log Book, Jack entered Flight Lieutenant Hoover as pilot, but this could have been out of habit. If it was a mistake, it would normally have been rectified at the end the month when the squadron commander signed the log book, but by the end of July, Wing

129

Commander Daniels had been replaced by Wing Commander Dixie Dean.

There was, however, another way of concentrating the impact of a bombing raid. Since their arrival in the European theatre, the Americans had bombed in daylight and in formation. There was no need to mark the target with flares because, cloud permitting, it could be seen, and the principle of concentration was maintained because the bombers remained in formation as they released their bombs. The RAF experimented with this approach and used it occasionally. Jack's views on the tactic are not revealed in his diary, which records only one such operation.

Tuesday 11th July 1944
(Op. 82)
A new thing in ops (for us). All the way there in formation and bombed in formation, led by Mosquito. Target P-Planes site at Gapennes near Abbeville. 10/10 cloud. Quiet trip. Duchess of Kent at interrogation on return.

Mosquito aircraft could fly higher than the German fighters and above flak, and they were thus used by the Pathfinders to drop the initial markers, using the latest radar equipment to help them identify the target. The squadron ORB record carries a conditional satisfaction with the results; in fact, Oboe was always very accurate:

Bombed on OBOE leader's release. Nothing seen of target. Bombing should be satisfactory if OBOEs were correct.

There is no record of whether any of Jack's crew talked with the Duchess of Kent.

Wednesday 12th July 1944
(Op. 83)
Night operations (D.M.B.) Bombing M/Y at Tours. An excellent trip. Map read way into Δ and marked very accurately. Bombing very well concentrated. Defences slight. Geoff's last trip.

Geoff Goom was the designated bomb-aimer in the crew, but he and Jack had been sharing the complex management of the bomb-aiming role. There is no record a permanent replacement for Sergeant Goom, but a replacement of some sort would be necessary given the high workload on the crew during the bombing phase of operations.

By his own account of the operations in June and July 1944, Jack seems to have taken the lead in all aspects of operations other than actually flying the aircraft. He was still acting as a volunteer bomb-aimer; he was responsible for radio communications; he was trained as a gunner should self-defence be required and now, it seems, he was doing the map-reading. He was also attracting the attention of his commanding officers, as we will soon see.

The squadron ORB provides good detail on the Tours raid on 12 July, for which the target was the extensive railway marshalling yard:

> Target identified visually by river bend to South and shape of marshalling yards, clearly seen. Red TIs were down on arrival and had undershot 500 yards SW of Aiming Point when MB's greens fell just South of Aiming Point on southern edge 15 seconds before our own green just overshooting aiming point to NE. At this time a few strings of flares had fallen overshooting the reds and giving good illumination, in response to the MB's direction to illuminate far side of reds. MB directed to 'bomb reds with 1 second overshoot'. Central part of marshalling yard then became obscured by smoke and MB directed Main Force to bomb east edge of smoke. As MB was giving clear instructions and had the attack well in hand, we left the target area immediately after bombing.

Four operations and eleven days before, we left General Montgomery still trying to break out past Caen. The 7 July raid had not been enough. A further massive bombing effort was needed to dislodge the enemy. Over 1,000 aircraft were committed to the operation, bombing five German positions, at Colombelles, Sannerville, Mondeville, Manneville and Cagny. Jack's target was at Manneville, which they reached at about 4.00 a.m. – around day-break. Wing Commander Daniels was his pilot, and they were detailed as master bomber. Air Chief

Marshal Sir Trafford Leigh-Mallory, Commander of the Allied Expeditionary Air Force, watched the raid from the air and recorded the sight in his diary,[10] as follows:

> The bombing of Bomber Command at first light was extraordinary. Aircraft were spread out in a great fan in the red dawn, coming in out over the sea. It was an incredible sight. Soon there was nothing but a pall of dust and smoke and I could see little from the Storch in which I was flying. I must say that air side was tremendously successful. The Army had been unable to move in the Caen area for three weeks and we got them unstuck in four hours. The Army were particularly cheerful to see the bombers going straight on through the flak undeviating towards their target. Occasionally one would go down in flames, but the others pressed on and never wavered. It was a magnificent sight.

The impact of the raid on the German forces was obtained from post-war interrogation of General Hans Eberbach, commander of Panzer Group West, again as recounted by Darlow:[11]

> The bomb carpet was a six kilometre square for the first time in their experience; all his rear areas and reserves were destroyed or disrupted...they got no word from the front for the rest of the day...his defence in depth served to hold...until 2000 hours when he got his first report from the front, and that of a breakthrough.

Debate on Montgomery's tactics at Caen continued long after the war was over, but there seems little doubt about the importance of the daylight raid on 18 July 1944. Leading this airborne armada (or at least its Manneville element) was the Commanding Officer of 35 Squadron, flying with what we can assume to be the crew he considered most suited for the job. The Squadron ORB records:

> MB, Pilot: Wg Daniels (OC 35 Squadron): DMB dropped white at 0051.30 hours; fell approx 500 yards overshoot. Main Force instructed to bomb starboard red target indicator. Bombing concentration appeared reasonable.

It is remarkable that whenever a commanding officer is on a raid, details from his debriefing always appear in the ORB. Jack in his diary seems almost laconic – just another job done well:

Tuesday 18th July 1944
(Op. 84)
Daylight raid with the C.O. Close Army support – Mannèville S.E. of Caen. Bombed and marked A/P. A very heavy concentrated raid. Lots of heavy flak – saw a/c go down in flames. Circled beachhead for ½ hour.
Normandy, reputedly a pretty part of France, looks badly scarred by war. Whole villages obliterated. C'est la guerre – if it's any comfort

Operating mainly at night, Jack would have seen little of the devastation of war. His observation on the condition of Normandy is as near as he comes to making a personal statement on the purpose and impact of war. He never stood on the soil of France, though he was to die there.

The Squadron ORB carries a record of the raid, and it indicates that Wing Commander Daniels and his crew were the master bomber, a detail not included in Jack's log book. It would have been Jack's bomb-aiming which started the battle. In the crew list he is still shown as a volunteer bomb-aimer, but he had, in fact, qualified as a bomb-aimer on the job.

The next three operations were over Germany, reverting to the strategic role.

Sunday 23rd July 1944
(Op. 85)
Germany again with night ops to Kiel. A decent trip but cloud over target – we retained our markers. Flak intense – no fighters or S/Lights.

It is not clear what the actual target was, but most likely it would be naval ships. This was the last occasion when Jack put a 'v' for volunteer after his crew role of bomb-aimer in his Flying Log Book. For his remaining five operations, if he survived them, he would be detailed as a qualified bomb-aimer.

Tuesday 25th July 1944
(Op. 86)

Target Stuttgart. We were told at the last moment that we were D.M.B., but when we got to target the M.B. failed to show so we did his duties – circled target for 25 minutes. A good effort and a nice trip for us. Saw a few a/c go down over Δ where there was quite a bit of flak and fighters.

There is no indication as to what happened to the designated master bomber. The need for a deputy is obvious. The squadron ORB gives a detailed summary of the raid which most likely originates in Hoover's crew debrief as they had to take over as master bomber:

Target identified on H2S, good picture confirmed by target indicators, then visually by railway and river. On first run dropped flares and bombs on centre of reds, a few greens down. One TI yellow seen. MB not heard so took over and instructed Main Force to bomb centre of all TIs. Insufficient flares dropped. Instruction to Main Force given as situation warranted. Main Force bombing improved with instruction. First TIs were N & NW of aiming point. Own TIs fell approx 200 yards South of aiming point. At first, bombing tended to undershoot. From approx 0207 a large column of smoke rising to about 5000 to 8000 ft was nearly obliterating TIs. Attack was good, concentration fair – slight wild bombing.

The RAF Graveley ORB is less enthusiastic:

The marking is reported to have been rather scattered, but it is thought that the weight of the bombing fell in the town and suburbs

It is difficult to correlate two such different reports. The most likely cause is that one report came from a crew who were over the target early in the raid when no instructions were available from the master bomber. It was certainly an expensive raid for Bomber Command: thirty-nine Lancasters were shot down. This did not deter HQ Bomber Command from designating Stuttgart as a target three nights later.

Friday 28th July 1944
   (Op. 87)
   Stuttgart again but this time there was cloud over Δ. Bombed through clouds and kept our markers. Lots of fighters around – saw lots of our a/c go down on the way there and back. We came all way back in cloud.

They could bomb through clouds only because of the development of the H2S radar. Apart from the technical challenges detailed in Chapter 9, the use of ground mapping radar by a bomber had some operational implications which the crew had to consider. Use of the radar would immediately reveal the location of the bomber to anyone who could identify the transmissions for what they were. A further disadvantage was that H2S only gave an accurate map when the aircraft was flying straight and level. For obvious reasons, bomber pilots preferred to twist and weave when over targets and when enemy night-fighters were about. The use of the H2S radar set was thus contentious. Eventually, it was generally agreed that the ability to see through cloud and thus to determine the exact location of the bomber out-weighed the disadvantages.

Friday 4th August 1944
   (Op. 88)
   An excellent daylight trip to the Gironde River (nr Bordeaux). Target an oil depot and refinery at Bec D'Ambes. We were M.B. and we marked A/P accurately. Over 100 a/c bombed in 9 mins and we saw tank after tank explode. At end of attack a column of black smoke rose from target to about 11,000 feet. No opposition – we had fighter escort on the way back. A very good show – as photographs proved.

A long sortie – seven and a half hours, all in daylight, – over France, with spectacular success. Again Jack refers to his photographs as evidence. The squadron ORB records the Master Bomber's debriefing:

One tank seemed to go up in a terrific explosion followed by a column of black smoke. Own TIs fell right on aiming point. Broadcast 'no cloud' and base at 8000 ft at 1755. Directed

Main Force to bomb on yellows at 18000 ft, and from 1803 onwards to bomb centre of smoke. At this time a huge column of black smoke was rising from centre of plant. Aircraft 'E' reported that no Master Bomber's instructions were heard and no target indicators seen.

The RAF Graveley ORB has similar reports, although it is not clear what happened to Aircraft 'E':

6 ac from 35 Squadron and 100 from 3 Group. All ac could see the target visually and the MB instructed the DMB to mark the A/P, following up with his own yellow TIs. The resultant attack was very successful and several large explosions were seen as the fuel tanks were hit and a huge column of smoke rose to approximately 10,000ft. Bombing was confined to the target area with very few exceptions. There was no opposition.

Flight Lieutenant Hoover and his crew were master bomber on the next raid also – a V1 storage depot. The campaign against the V1 threat had become more fruitful since the bombers were sent to the storage depots rather than the launch sites. Since early July there had been a steady reduction in the number of V1 launches against London, sufficient to ensure that the German strategic aim of terrorising the population of London was not achieved.

Sunday 6th August 1944
(Op. 89)
P-Planes site again in daylight at the Foret de Nieppes, France. (M/B). Oboe TI 1000yds off. Ours down on A/P but bombing by M/F not so good. Stayed in area 15 mins, directing attack which was half successful.

That was Jack's 89th operation – just one more to go, and he appears to have enjoyed it. His squadron's ORB records the crew debrief, as follows:

Target identified by Target Indicator red and visually by canal and railway. Target Indicators red seen going down at approximately -4 which fell on extreme Eastern edge of target. Another extreme. Another one at -2 (minutes) South of aiming point 400 yards. Own target indicators, green, fell almost 'bang-on' aiming point which was identified by the light of flames. One huge explosion seen at 2333. After green went down instructed Main Force to bomb it, later to bomb between green and red. The explosion was between green and red and then instructed to bomb explosion. Smoke then obscuring target and instructions given to bomb target indicators, green, up to H+6.

No other 35 Squadron aircraft was on this raid.

There is a similar record in the RAF Graveley ORB:

The MB saw a red TI which fell on the Eastern edge of the target followed by another 400 yards South of A/P. He identified the target easily by the light of flames and dropped his own TIs on the A/P. Crews were instructed to bomb the green and a large explosion was seen at 2333. Later, crews were instructed to bombs positions East of an explosion which emanated between the green and red to the East. Target then became obscured but bombing continued on green until H+6.

We now come to Jack's last 'op', it is only fair to let him have the last word on his operational flying:

Tuesday 8th August 1944
(Op. 90)
Did a 'one-man' PFF job tonight. Supposed to be D.M.B but M.B. had trouble and didn't take off and we took over. Impossible to see ground in Δ area so we dropped flares and came in again to mark A/P accurately with green T.I. Then we directed bombing which was very good – well concentrated. A tremendous explosion at +6 and burning still visible when we were 80 miles away. The target, by the way, was petrol and oil dump at Aire-sur-Lys.
My 90th.

He nearly forgot to say what the target was. Remembering that only he knew about his diary, and there is no evidence that anyone else read it before it came to light in 1992, Jack's 'one-man PFF job' can be taken only as it reads – on that night he directed the bombing and took tactical charge of the whole raid. Evidence from those who knew him, and passed on their views, is that Jack Mossop was in all aspects a modest man, more interested in doing a job well than talking about it. However, the feeling of a job well done is clear in this, his last entry in his Collins Aero diary for 1944.

Over 100,000 men flew in Bomber Command. Over half were killed.[12] A table drawn up by the Air Ministry in November 1942 shows that in a heavy bomber squadron the chance of surviving one tour was 44 per cent.[13] If the level of risk remained the same the chances of surviving three tours is around 8 per cent. It is probable that risk during a tour of operations in 1944 and 1945 was less than in previous years, so is possibly more accurate to suggest that Jack had survived odds of around 12 per cent, or one in eight, in completing his three tours.

On 15 August 1944 Air Vice-Marshal Bennett, Air Officer Commanding 8 Group, signed the certificate which awarded Jack a Pathfinder Force Badge on a permanent basis. He had been entitled to wear the badge since soon after 35 Squadron but the badge was only awarded on a permanent basis to those who completed a full tour on a Pathfinder squadron.

On 21 November 1944 Jack was summoned to Buckingham Palace where he received both his first and his second DFC from King George VI. He was accompanied by Hilda and his sister Mary. The citation for the second DFC reads:

Act. Flt. Lt. J. Mossop, D.F.C., D.F.M., R.A.F.V.R., No. 35 Squadron. – Flt. Lt. Mossop has completed a very large number of operational sorties. He has proved himself to be an ideal leader. His skill, courage, and determination to reach his objective have contributed very largely to the fine record of success achieved by his crew and the excellent photographic evidence obtained.

The same issue of the London Gazette also carried the citation for Flight Lieutenant Hoover's second DFC:

This officer is an outstanding pilot and captain of aircraft. He has completed numerous night operations against the enemy and has at all times pressed home his attacks in spite of enemy opposition. Flight Lieutenant Hoover has displayed great tenacity and determination to achieve his objective, and his skill, courage and coolness in action have set a fine example to his crew.

Hoover had, of course, not completed ninety operations when Jack left the crew. He had in fact only done fifty-six. As he leaves our story here, it is appropriate to record briefly his further flying career.

As 1944 reached its climax in delivering the victories which would become the stepping stones to winning the war, the RAF was for the first time able to meet its own requirements for trained aircrew without support from its Allies. In particular, the secondment of RCAF aircrew to the RAF was no longer necessary, and they were taken back into their own service. Soon after Jack had left his crew, Hoover himself left 35 Squadron and was posted back to his homeland. He had a frustrating two months at a holding camp near to Manchester waiting for a sea passage across the Atlantic, but having reached Canada he was posted as an instructor on Liberator aircraft. After the war ended Hoover was de-mobilised on 8 September 1945. However, this was not the end of his military career. When the Cold War began to dominate international relations both the British and the Canadian governments again saw the need for strong air forces, and the RAF asked its NATO ally for assistance in training pilots. A recruiting drive was launched, and on 15 September 1954 Flight Lieutenant Hoover volunteered and rejoined the RCAF as a pilot, on a short service engagement of five years, which was, however, extended. He was again posted to UK, where he did a study on the training needs of pilots. He also taught in RAF Flying Training Command for 2½ years, at RAF Stations Binbrook, Lindholme and Marham where he was a member of the Central Bomber Establishment. He had re-joined in the rank of Flying Officer, and he was promoted to Flight Lieutenant (for the second time) on 6 June 1955. He had one more promotion, to squadron leader on 6 August 1965, and he remained a serving officer until 14 September 1970.[14] After leaving the air force he went to live in the Richmond area of Vancouver.

139

Chapter 11

Was It All Worth It?

Much has been said and written on the military value of the bomber offensive, its cost to the Allies in men and machines, and its impact on the course of the war; so much that it is possible to find substantive but perhaps selective evidence to support almost any view which may be put forward. I do not wish to dwell on the issue here, because I have no doubt that Jack and many like him simply knew that the United Kingdom and the British Commonwealth and their Allies faced a strong and menacing threat to their freedom. They were not born to be warriors, although their parents had faced a similar threat in 1914. In both world wars victory was the only acceptable conclusion. There was little that a twenty year old print operator could do other than to volunteer. Jack and thousands of others accepted the risk, perhaps fortunate that they did not know how poor the odds of survival actually were. After that, events took their course. The cost and benefit equation can be expressed in many ways, but here I will take a simplified view.

First, the costs. Much of the UK's arms manufacturing capability was taken up by the production and support of aircraft and other equipment for the armed forces. However, this effort was in due course largely shouldered by the USA and Canada. Furthermore, wartime research and development gave the UK a good platform for munitions sales after the war. Whether this advantage was realised is questionable, but the opportunity was there. However, a society is at risk from many factors in addition to the financial cost of war. The loss of human lives is much more significant. As we have seen, the Mossop family was split asunder by the war, as were hundreds of thousands of other families. During the Second World War over 70,000 RAF aircrew were killed in action, of which about 55,000 were from Bomber Command. Furthermore, about 5,500 bomber aircrew were lost in training and other accidents. What did they achieve at such a cost? I will attempt to measure some of their achievement, but first let me say that a comparison with casualties in other military campaigns is a sterile activity. For example, the 120,000 British soldiers killed in the first Battle of the Somme in 1916 and the very similar number of German soldiers killed in the same battle, fell in part because of barren tactics and a failure to recognise the value of advancing technology, particularly in that example the use of tanks. Bomber Command aircrew faced danger every time they flew, but they knew that they had as their tools of battle the best equipment which could be provided and a command chain which gave them confidence.

So much for the costs. What about the benefits? It is useful first to consider a view from the other side. In 1965 a German author, Hans Dollinger, compiled a reasoned and well-researched set of statistics and views in his book *The Decline and Fall of Nazi Germany and Imperial Japan*.[1] Although the statistics do not provide direct answers, they at least provide a perspective of the question hanging over the bomber offensive.

Quoting from a US Bombing Survey of September 1945, Dollinger gives the overall cost in personnel and matériel of the British and American effort as follows:

Allied Air Forces at the height of the attack threw 28,000 aircraft and 1,335,000 men into the struggle against Germany. More than 1,440,000 bomber and 2,680,000 fighter sorties were flown. The U.S. lost 79,265 and the U.K. 79,281 men during these sorties. More than 18,000 U.S. and 22,000 British aircraft were lost or damaged beyond repair.

The German authorities kept good records of the impact of the bombing campaign. Throughout Germany, 593,000 people were killed in air raids. In Frankfurt alone, air raids killed 5,559 people, 1,001 of them in a single night, 22 March 1944. As it happens, that was Jack's first raid with 35 Squadron, Op. 55, the night the 'nav boobed', and Bomber Command lost twenty-two bombers and 154 aircrew. Dollinger provides a rationale for night raids on German cities:

> At the beginning of the war, the RAF experimented briefly with daylight raids and discovered that the losses did not justify them. Next they tried night raids only to find that, in the dark, it was impossible to locate works or installations with sufficient accuracy to obtain satisfactory results. Early in 1942, they therefore had recourse to the systematic pattern bombing of German towns providing a large target. From October 1939 to May 1945, the RAF dropped more than half a million tons of high explosive, incendiary, and fragmentation bombs on 61 German towns each with a population of more than 100,000. The total population of these towns was 25 million (32 per cent of all Germans) and included nearly 5 million workers.

There is much truth in this rationale. 1942 was a difficult year for Britain. Not so much because of direct enemy action; indeed, the seeds of victory had been sown with the Japanese attack on Pearl Harbor and Hitler's attack on the USSR. But the Russians were facing an invasion which would cost them nearly 5 million casualties, and the Americans were still mobilising. It was clear to the British Government that the war could only be won through alliances with the USA and the USSR, but it had no means of taking the fight to the enemy. Defensive campaigns to hold Malaya, Singapore and Burma had failed, Allied shipping losses in the Atlantic were at their height, and the Russians were falling back to Moscow. Calls for Britain to open a second front in Europe could not be entertained, simply because Britain, on its own, did not have the required resources. The only option facing Britain was to resort to a strategic bombing campaign. The purpose was as much to encourage the leaders of the USA and the USSR as it was to demonstrate to the leaders of Germany and Italy that the UK would not shirk the fight.

The conduct of the bomber offensive was necessarily conditioned by what was possible. But what was possible was by no means derisory. If we take the proportion of workers in the overall population of bombed cities indicated in Dollinger's rationale quoted above, about 120,000 workers in German's industrial towns died as a result of bombing. Dollinger quotes from *Zwischen Krieg und Frieden* (*Between War and Peace*) by Feis to illustrate the extent of physical damage suffered by Germany, as follows:

> The most serious material damage was the destruction of houses, factories, offices and stores, particularly in the larger cities. The extent of this damage is illustrated by the fact that on average ten Germans now live where only four had lived in 1939; moreover, some of the cellars which they occupy hardly deserve the name of dwellings. The German railway was a heap of rubble. Not a single one of the inland watercourses, which had carried a large proportion of the German goods traffic, was intact. Coal and steel production was at less then 10 per cent of pre-war levels.

Justifying battle in terms of numbers killed is not pleasant, but any retrospective consideration of the validity of the British government's decision to launch the strategic bombing campaign has to consider the impact it had on German resources. The loss of work capacity, the disruption of transport, the lack of matériel resources necessary to maintain the war effort, the diversion of the armed forces to the air defence system and to fire fighting and rescue services, would each on their own provide justification for the bomber offensive, at least as far as any battle can be justified. The reduction in steel production might alone justify the effort. Perhaps we can leave the final word on the issue to an American. Dollinger's book has a forward written by Lieutenant General Ira C. Eaker, who was the Commanding General of the United States Eighth Air Force in England from 1942 to 1944. It includes a paragraph which only a no-nonsense American general could write:

> Those miniwits who now prate about the ineffectiveness of air power obviously never saw Berlin or Tokyo and never served on a battlefield or a fleet under hostile aircraft.[2]

By 1945, wider strategic factors had arisen. It became evident

143

that the USSR was intent on occupying as much of Germany as it could, along with other countries in Eastern Europe. The final assault on Berlin was not a tactical battle. The RAF and the USAAF continued to bombard Berlin, even when it was clear that the war was won. What mattered in 1945 was who would dominate Europe. The first prize went to the Soviet Union, but the Western powers had done enough to join their errant ally on the rostrum. Throughout the six years of war, RAF Bomber Command had taken the fight to the enemy. At times, it had been the only Allied command able to do so. There had been much to learn about the demands of such a long and arduous campaign, and many setbacks, but at the end no one doubted that the sacrifice had been necessary.

Similar credit, of course, is due to the other commands of the RAF. Fighter Command had won its spurs early in the war during the Battle of Britain, whilst the long battle over the Atlantic against the submarine threat had tested Coastal Command. I have no doubt that the RAF deserved the soubriquet bestowed on it by John Terraine in his book of that name:[3] *The Right of the Line*. This was the honour bestowed by King Edward III on his son, the sixteen year old Black Prince after the Battle of Crécy in 1346. The vanguard on the right of the English line of battle at Crécy was the place of greatest danger. The young prince held the line, and the heavily outnumbered English army eventually won the day. So did the RAF hold the line, through six hard years of a war unlike any previously fought.

Chapter 12

A New Horizon

Ninety operations was the limit. Only one or two exceptional pilots such as Guy Gibson and Leonard Cheshire persuaded the authorities that they might do more. As a WOP/AG with a bomb-aimer qualification, Jack's future was in the training units. He might have gained a permanent commission in the RAF and forged out a useful career. But an alternative course emerged.

His posting from 35 Squadron on 5 November 1944 was to No. 1663 Heavy Conversion Unit at Rufforth, in Yorkshire, where he was a wireless telegraphy instructor. Some aircrew had a perverse fear of non-operational flying because they felt it created more risk than operations. The basis of this concern was that aircraft in the training role seemed to crash regularly. What they did not see, of course, was the much larger number of aircraft which were lost on operations. Jack flew in Halifax aircraft as part of his instructional duties about once a week, but he was at Rufforth for only five weeks. In early October he was posted to RAF Chigwell on signals officer duties, and then, on 2 April 1945, he was posted to the Lancaster Finishing School (LFS) at RAF Ossington, which is about six miles north-west of Newark-on-Trent. The school had been set up early in 1944 as a sort of finishing school for new Lancaster crews. Jack had a few sorties as an instructor, but Ossington had another role, which was the main purpose of Jack's posting.

As the war neared its end, air-minded people in government had noted the war-driven development of long range four-engined aircraft. If the UK was to assume again the worldwide influence it previously enjoyed before 1939 it would need air routes to facilitate international business. The British Overseas Airways Corporation (BOAC) and British European Airways Corporation (BEA) had been formed with government assistance. A new airliner, the Lancastrian, based on the design of the Lancaster bomber, was in production, and there was also a fleet of York passenger aircraft. What they lacked was sufficient aircrew to provide a worldwide service. The RAF and the RAFVR had the opposite problem: with the end of conflict in sight, there would not be the need for all the aircrew currently in uniform. The solution was simple: lend aircrew to the airlines and encourage them to take up employment in civil aviation.

On 27 March 1945, Jack was summoned to Room 736 in Alexandra House in Kingsway, London, there to face at 10.00 a.m. a board who would determine his future. The following day at 8.30 a.m. he attended on Wing Commander O'Brien in Imperial House, also in Kingsway, for a medical examination. Most likely on the same day, he also had an interview with Wing Commander Hazelman in Adastral House, presumably to arrange the RAF's acquiescence to Jack's secondment. The bureaucracy involved in Jack's transfer seems to have been remarkably simple. He was asked to complete a short form, so short that it would fit on a piece of paper less than A5 in size, and he had to take to the Board his Flying Log Book, his Pay Book, and Form 657 or 'any other evidence of medical category'. The details to be completed on the form were:

1. Date and place of Aircrew Selection Board, to which Jack responded: 'approx May 1940 – RAF Watton', at which time he was actually well into his basic trade training at No. 3 E & WS.

2. All courses attended, date, place, and marks. Jack contented himself with only three courses, no doubt those he thought the most relevant to his new employment: his W/Op course which finished Yatesbury on 3 December 1940, his gunnery course which finished at Penhros on 1 February 1941 and his Operations Training Course which finished at Cottesmore on 16 June 1941. Gunnery and most of his operations training would have little relevance to civilian flying, so

146

presumably Jack was recruited on the basis of his wireless operating skills.

3. A short proforma which can easily be re-produced:

Date of Birth 17/4/20	Seniority in present rank 9/9/43	Date of Enlistment 4/4/40	
Operational Aircraft Flown(recent types first)	*Squadron or Unit*	*Total Flying times on each type of operational aircraft*	
Lancaster	35 (PFF)	205.25	
Halifax II & V	76 Squadron + NTU, 1664, + 1652	222.00	
Hampden	49 Squadron + NTU	342.10	
Whitley	Gunnery school + 10 OTU	25.10	
Wellington	16 OTU, 10 OTU	16.00	
Date of last sortie August 8th 1944	*Last operational command* Bomber – 8(PFF) Gp	*Total operational hours* 500	*Total flying hours* 936.50
Medical Category A3B	*Date and place of last Medical Board* 5/3/5 – RAF Catterick		

Again, it must be observed that the relevance and pith of this form suggests an organisation not overburdened by bureaucracy. Jack did not seem to be too concerned over it. The figures he gave for operational and total flying hours are none too accurate. My reckoning of his total flying hours as recorded in his log book is 1,297, about 40 per cent more than he declared on this form.

Ossington's other role was to convert military aircrew into civilian aircrew. Its syllabus was mainly ground based, largely dealing with the procedural aspects of civilian flying. However, with the end of hostilities, some of the more pleasurable aspects of military life were permissible. An invitation card from the Officer Commanding RAF Station Ossington requested the pleasure of 'Mrs J. Mossop's company at a Mess Dance on Saturday 26th May 1945, at 8pm'. Dress was optional. The officers would be in uniform, but it would have been unfair on the ladies to expect them to have ball gowns after five years of wartime restrictions. Hilda would have enjoyed the dancing, and Jack would have had to pretend to do so. Details of the buffet menu are written in Jack's handwriting on the back of the invitation card: Chicken..Pork..Ham..Salad..Tomatoes..Scotch Eggs..Ice Cream – hardly a feast to mark the end of the most destructive war in history.

Having arrived early in April 1945, Jack did not fly at Ossington until 21 June. That flight did, however, provide an appropriate finale to his military flying career, because for the first and only time he saw the Ruhr Valley in daylight. Given his many nocturnal visits to the Ruhr this must have been a flight of both nostalgia and relief. It was also the only time that he flew in a Dakota; an American passenger aircraft which, for some years, would prove too much of a challenge for the British aircraft industry, then trying to convert back to civilian requirements, after a long period during which military requirements had taken priority.

Jack then had five local flights in Lancasters before setting off to learn the route to Rabat, on the west coast of Morocco. The first stage was short, to Hurn aerodrome, near Bournemouth, where BOAC was then based. Hurn to Rabat on 10 July took 6½ hours. The return leg on 12 July had to be aborted because of a problem with an engine one hour after taking off. A replacement Lancaster was found and Jack was back at Ossington on 15 July. He finished the course on 15 July 1945, and on 31 July he was formally seconded to BOAC as a Radio Officer. He was to be based at Hurn airport, and he rented a flat in the Branksome Park area of Bournemouth. Jack, Hilda and Bill, who was now six months old, lived together for the first time. Although he had been guaranteed one week on leave every six weeks when still at Graveley, that had only amounted to two weeks since his honeymoon. Married quarters were hard to come by on the training units, and leave was no longer guaranteed. They had managed some weekends together, but they had not lived together at all as a conventional family. Since their marriage, Hilda had continued to work in Newcastle upon Tyne, and she continued to live with her parents. When Jack did get leave he stayed with them. Fortunately his parents-in-law thought the world of Jack, which was just as well as he had married their younger daughter, and Stags Head cottage in Medomsley was the only home which Hilda and young Bill had known (not that I knew much about it at the time). But now he was taking them away from her family. Hilda gave up her job in Newcastle, and two weeks after Jack left Ossington, having moved his family to Bournemouth, he was away on his first overseas flight with BOAC.

Airline journeys in those days were measured in days rather than hours. As an example, on his first trip Jack left Hurn on 16 August and arrived at Karachi, on 21 August having staged through Malta, Cairo and Shaiba. Then he returned along the same route, reaching Hurn on 25 August. The compensation was that the next overseas flight was not until 14 September. In between flights he was called in for air tests and other local flying. On 21 February 1946 he was ferried to Croydon in an Airspeed Oxford, a twin engined training aircraft flown on this occasion by Flying Officer Barnes, to make up a crew so that Captain Griffiths could bring a BOAC Avro York back to Hurn. The York was a passenger aircraft similar size to a Lancastrian. However, having been designed for passengers from the beginning, the York could carry twenty-four passengers. On the other hand, the York did not have the range of the Lancastrian, 2,700 miles against the Lancastrian's 4,150. BOAC had a fleet of Yorks at Hurn, and Jack flew just over half his hours with BOAC in York aircraft. Most of the remainder were in Lancastrians. For the first time since they met, Hilda could expect Jack home at reasonably predictable times. Even the overseas flights, which were often delayed by weather and other factors, brought benefits. Jack was able to bring back some simple comforts of life which were not available or affordable in post-war Britain – eggs, for example were rationed in Britain but easily available in Egypt. Even luxuries such as Turkish cigarettes could be brought home.

Jack flew down the routes to Delhi, Calcutta, Karachi, and Johannesburg, usually from Hurn, but sometimes from the newly opened London Airport at Heathrow. Before the Second World War, London's main civil airport was at Croydon, but during the war Heathrow became more favoured because of its greater scope for development. New runways had been laid down during 1944, and Heathrow officially opened for civil air movements on 31

May 1946 when a BOAC Lancastrian flew in from Australia. Facilities for both crew and passengers were rather primitive. When it opened, the terminal could only offer a series of tents containing armchairs, a bar, chemical toilets, and a shop selling books and newspapers. However, in its first year of operation, the airport handled about 60,000 passengers and about 9,000 aircraft movements.[1]

On Saturday 30 June 1946, Jack flew with Captain Key to position a Lancastrian at London Heathrow prior to a flight to Karachi. He wrote a letter to Hilda from London where he was staying overnight in the Coburg Court Hotel at 129 Bayswater Road, near to Hyde Park. This is the only letter which Hilda kept.

My Darling,

As you will see, I am at yet another different place. It is near Marble Arch – not bad but I would prefer the hotel we stayed at in Windsor.

I told you just before we left that we were due back on the Tuesday but now it seems that that it is to be Monday after all – it will be latish in the evening – in fact if we are very late we may stay up here overnight and fly down on the Tuesday morning.

There has been terrific rainfall up here – I hope it doesn't delay your Mum and Dad – they should be well on their way to Bournemouth now – I hope the weather improves for them.

Last night a bunch of us (seven in all – both crews are staying here) went on a pub crawl around the West End. We didn't get an awful lot of beer as most places were on the point of selling out but it was good fun – I didn't get around to the Pathfinder Club. It was after midnight when I got to bed so I gave up the idea of meeting Mum and Dad at K.X.[2]

By the way, I phoned – or tried to – last night – couldn't get through – maybe some of the lines were down due to the storm.

Well, my darling, I will be on my way shortly. Don't worry about me. I will be thinking about you (as I wing my way southward!!). I have your photograph – I love you, Hilda, my darling more than anything in the world – you are my world always remember that, darling, please. Goodbye until Monday (or Tuesday) week.

The letter concludes romantically.

By the following midday Jack was on his way to Karachi staging through Lydda in what was then Palestine, about twenty miles from Jerusalem, and now called Lod, the site of Tel Aviv airport. London to Lydda was a long stage in propeller driven aircraft. They logged 7½ hours in daylight and 4¼ hours at night. However, they did not leave Lydda until 3 July, so they may have had time to visit Jerusalem. He got home on the Monday, two weeks later. Hilda's parents and Ethel, Hilda's elder sister, had all arrived safely, and the sky had cleared. The small beaches which run west from Bournemouth are known as chines. Branksome Chine is only a few minutes walk from the flat which Jack had rented. The sun shone, and the photographs taken that week seem almost to justify the war. The successes of 1944 were, at last, bearing fruit, rather than mere laurels.

The war was over, and the RAFVR was being stood down. Jack could either request transfer to the RAF or look for other employment. He chose the latter and was offered a job by BOAC. His last day of RAFVR service was on 19 August 1946. He had served his King for six years, five months, and fifteen days. Twice he had been to Buckingham Palace to receive medals, on the first occasion his DFM, and on the second occasion to receive his two DFCs. On handing them over, King George VI said 'I see you have been here before'.

During his last two weeks as a commissioned officer in the RAFVR Jack was entitled to terminal leave, a term which I have always seen as somewhat unfortunate. However, Jack took his family back to Medomsley, and he survived his terminal leave. He and Hilda returned to their flat on 18 August 1946, the day before he ceased to be an officer in the Royal Air Force Volunteer Reserve. Waiting for Jack at their flat was a note asking if he could, at short notice, make up the crew on a training flight. The following day he reported to Hurn airfield and boarded Lancastrian G-AGMF as the instructor wireless operator on a trip to Karachi, staging through Lydda on the outbound and the inbound legs.

Chapter 13

Lancastrian G-AGMF

The exigencies of a desperate war had created anomalies in the development and manufacture of aircraft and other industrial products. The UK and the USA had agreed that the Americans would concentrate on transport aircraft while the British would concentrate on fighters and bombers. During 1944, however, it became clear to the British Government that the advances in aviation brought about both during, and because of, the war would give a significant advantage to both manufacturers of transport aircraft and to civilian airlines in the USA. There was no passenger aircraft produced in UK which could meet the requirements of a long-range airliner. The big bombers could carry heavy loads, and they had a long range, but they had little by way of even the minimal comforts expected by passengers.

In an attempt to overcome this deficiency, through the issue of Specification C. 16/44 the British Air Ministry had asked the manufacture of the Lancaster to produce a civilian version with a licence to carry civilian passengers. As an encouragement, the RAF would buy sixty-four of the aircraft for military require- ments. The Lancastrian, as it was called, was a new type, albeit based on the Lancaster and using the same Rolls-Royce Merlin engines.   The first batch to be delivered was designated Lancastrian Mark 1. Twenty-three aircraft were taken off the Lancaster production line and were converted into airliners. The Lancastrian Mark 1 could cruise at around 310mph at 12,000ft and it had a range of over 4,000 miles. Its main disadvantage was its low capacity – it could seat only nine passengers, although they also got a bunk each in which to sleep. BOAC bought thirty

Mark 1 Lancastrians for use on the so-called Kangaroo service to Australia. BOAC crews flew them as far as Karachi, where Qantas crews took over for the legs to Australia and back. In BOAC service the standard crew was two pilots, one navigator, one wireless operator and two stewards. The Mark 2 version of the Lancastrian was a military version of the Mark 1 produced for the RAF. British South American Airways (BSAA) received six Lancastrians in the Mark 3 version, out of an initial order for eighteen aircraft. Reducing the size of the crew accommodation, and other weight reduction measures, enabled the Mark 3 Lancastrians to take thirteen passengers. The last version of the Lancastrian, the Mark 4, was a military version of the Mark 3. In all, only eighty-two Lancastrians were built.[1]

The Lancastrian had a poor in-service safety record. By 1950, there had been twenty-two reportable occurrences, of which six involved fatalities – a BSAA aircraft crashed onto a glacier the Andes and has only recently been found, and another fell into the Indian Ocean en route to Australia, with no survivors. However, there was no evidence of technical failings as the cause of crashes, although the RAF Pilot's Notes for the Lancastrian[2] contains a flying limitation which could have had relevance to some of these accidents:

Care must be taken to avoid imposing excessive loads with the elevators in recovering from dives and in turns at high speed.

The crew which Jack had so swiftly joined when returning from leave consisted of two pilots, two navigators, two radio operators, and two stewards:

Captain J.R.G. Copeland

First Officer d'A. Sephton

Navigating Officer L.R. Hastings

Navigating Officer G.F. Winbury

Radio Officer Mossop

Radio Officer Blades

Steward F.W. Roberts

Steward K.L. Bloxham

The purpose of the flight was to check out newly qualified officers. Sephton, Winbury and Blades had all passed the courses in their respective aircrew disciplines, but they needed a route check before they could fly with passengers. The route in question was from Hurn to Karachi and back, staging through Lydda in each direction. Captain Copeland had received a memorandum from the captain of 'A' Flight at Hurn stating that First Officer Sephton was to operate in command of the training flight. Copeland was, at his own discretion, to allow Sephton the maximum opportunity to handle the aircraft and 'freedom of decision'. More significantly, Sephton was to be caused to show his capabilities as opportunities occurred. It is not clear exactly what was meant by this. It was Sephton's first flight in supervised command, and it seems that he was to be given the opportunity to make the appropriate decisions should any unexpected circumstance arise.

Jack was already an old hand on intercontinental passenger flights and had flown down this particular route twelve times previously. His only responsibility on this occasion was to monitor the performance of Radio Officer Blades. On the return journey, Jack wrote out his notes on the performance of his student in pencil, as follows:

R/O Blades

Lanc. Training Flight

G\AGMF

Telegraphy -Fair

Log-keeping – Poor

Knowledge of Route – Incomplete

This R/O seemed to be quite keen and, as he gets more experience should be fairly efficient. At present his faults are:

Slowness on the key and Morse sending not too good.

An incomplete knowledge of facilities available.

A lamentable habit of trying to hold lots of stuff in his head, then filling in his log at his leisure.

He seems to try to overcome this.

Recommended – that he should be passed out for service. I think he may work better when alone.

Signed
Mossop R/O

It can be seen that Jack's pragmatism had not been left behind with the RAF. The role of the radio officer in a civilian airliner was less demanding than that of a wireless operator in a heavy bomber, but it was critical to safety. With flights in excess of twelve hours it was essential that any variations in the weather forecast made prior to departure were made available to crews in flight. The aircraft were not pressurised and thus could not fly at high level, above the effects of the weather. Their navigators also lacked equipment which would allow precision in knowing their position. Dead reckoning was based on an assumption that the aircraft's course and speed over the ground had been accurately maintained. In a long distance flight, the pilot and navigator needed updates on the wind speed and direction en route, and the pilot would need to know the local weather conditions at the destination airfield, and at any diversion airfield. It was the task of the radio officer to obtain this information using wireless telegraphy and Morse code.

The outbound journey was uneventful. They stayed overnight in accommodation at Lydda airfield before flying on to Karachi. There was an Officer's Club at Tel Aviv, where Jack had stayed at least once, on 14 February 1946. A photograph taken in the club bar on that occasion shows Jack, Captain Holdaway, First Officer

155

Pete Harding and a navigator identified only as 'Pete'. On other occasions Jack had visited Jerusalem. He had made some purchases at The New Market Store run by Nizar I.B. Attieh and F. Dakkak opposite the Convent of St Abraham, near the Church of the Holy Sepulchre, in the Old City. He had also brought home as a souvenir a leaf from one of the trees in the Garden of Gethsemane, glued into a folded piece of paper on which was written in English a prayer for the dying. In a sense, Jack had himself been dying during his flying career, as the time dimension of the risk equation lengthened. The risk exposure was, of course, particularly high during his three operational tours in Bomber Command because of the nature of the hazardous events to which he had been exposed. Time's wallet had been enlarged for Jack. The hazard level was much lower in civilian flying, but the clock still ticked. Almost certainly, like others who did not flinch when facing danger, Jack would not have seen personal risk as a quantity which can be measured.

On this occasion, Jack was confined to Lydda airfield because of another type of hazard which he had probably not previously confronted. The State of Israel had not then been formed and the UK was responsible under a League of Nations mandate for government in what was still called Palestine. But some of the Jews already in Palestine did not accept that the formation of the new state of Israel was being progressed as they wished. There had been an escalation in violence caused by the tension between the British, Jewish and Arab forces. British property was subjected to terrorist attacks. On 22 July 1946, only one month previous to Jack's staging through Lydda on G-AGMF, a militant Zionist group, Irgun, had exploded bombs in the King David Hotel in Jerusalem, which at the time was being used as the headquarters of the British Secretariat. Ninety-two people, twenty-eight of them British, forty-one Arab, seventeen Jewish and five others were killed.[3] There had been a telephoned warning which should have been long enough to evacuate the building, but the reaction was too slow. All seven storeys of one wing of the hotel were destroyed. BOAC reacted by restricting their staff to the airfield at Lydda.

Some of crew of G-AGMF knew quite a lot about the bombing of buildings, but they were no longer in that trade. They flew on to Karachi without incident, and then they turned round and set off for home. They were again confined to base when staging through Lydda. The aircraft was given a routine check-out by the Lydda BOAC technical staff. Captain Copeland reported one minor defect, a hydraulic leak below his seat. This was potentially serious as it could prevent use of the flaps, but the cause was traced to a union on one of the flap selectors and it was rectified by tightening the union. The repair was confirmed by a two hour test, after which the union was found still to be dry. With the hydraulic oil leak fixed, Copeland obtained a weather report which forecast fine weather as far as Sardinia, where showers and multiple levels of cloud could be expected as they neared the south coast of France. This cumulonimbus cloud could reach an altitude of 20,000 feet, giving the possibility of icing as they flew over southern France. The worst of the weather was, therefore, expected to be between Malta and Marseilles. On this final leg back to Hurn they had a passenger, Mr W.J. Smith, who was an operations officer employed by BOAC at Lydda. He was travelling home for a period of leave.

The small town of Broglie in northern France lies some seventy-two miles (115 km) east of Paris and twenty-seven miles (forty-three km) from the English Channel north of Le Havre. The nearest large town is Bernay, about six miles (nine km) to the north-east. This is the part of France which Jack had written about in his diary following Op. 84; the Army support operation at Manneville on 18 July 1944:

> Normandy, reputedly a pretty part of France, looks badly scarred by war. Whole villages obliterated. C'est la guerre – if it's any comfort

Manneville is only about forty miles (sixty kms) from Broglie. The war had passed through the area some two years previously and rural France had largely recovered from its impact. Its small villages surrounded by farms in a rolling countryside are typical of northern France. St Aubin-du-Thenney, a little over a mile from Broglie, is such a village. The apple trees had recovered from whatever damage the war had caused two years before, cider was back in full production and livestock had returned to

157

near normal levels. Louis Leblond, a forty year old baker lived in Broglie, and he was, as usual, up early on 20 August 1946. By 6 a.m. he was at work ensuring that his employer's oven was hot enough to bake the first bread of the day. At 6.15 a.m. he heard an unusual sound; an aircraft which he thought was flying low and circling the town. He left the oven and looked outside, where he saw an aircraft flying in flames over Broglie Castle.

Eugene Carel was another early riser, or possibly he had not yet got to bed. He also saw the aircraft as he walked home to Broglie from Chamblac. He had reached Bilhaudiere, about two kilometres from Broglie, when he saw it approaching low from the east. He could not tell whether the engines were running correctly, but within only a few seconds he saw a flash and smoke rising from the ground. Carel immediately informed the French National Constabulary, and the local chief of police and three constables set out to find the wreckage. They found it about 1,500 metres (one mile) to the west of Broglie.

Maurice Legas had also been up early on 20 August. He was an upholsterer who also lived in Broglie. He had set out at 6 a.m. to go to the village of St Aubin-du-Thenney, walking along the D49 road. He had only reached the edge of the town when he heard the aircraft. At first he could not see it because of mist, but then he saw it crash ahead of him into a field belonging to Beauvais Farm. He did not see flames before it crashed. The fire and explosions started after it had bounced along the ground, breaking apple trees as it skidded to a stop.

Pierre Despinoy, the caretaker at Beauvais Farm, was still in his bed when, at 6.15 a.m., he heard a noise of an aircraft which seemed to be flying at a very low altitude. He got out of bed just in time to see it, apparently in difficulty, flying at tree-top level. He rushed to the back of his house, but by the time he got there the aircraft had crashed in a field about 500 yards away. There was a big explosion, followed by flames.

The noise of an aircraft in difficulty had also been heard at 6.15 a.m. by Pierre Bouillier, a market gardener who lived nearby. He had still been in bed but he soon got up to see a thick cloud of smoke rising from the Beauvais Farm field. He too rushed to the site of the accident. As he approached, he met Pierre Despinoy and Maurice Legas, who were trying to extricate injured

158

occupants from the wreckage. Immediately recognising the need to get the injured to hospital, Pierre Bouillier went back to fetch his car, in which he conveyed two people to Bernay hospital, a distance of about five miles. It was obvious to him that one of two injured was in a serious condition.

Pierre Despinoy then telephoned his boss, Michel Loncke, who lived at Tournedos-Bois-Hubert. He was the farmer who rented the fields into which the aircraft had crashed. Loncke came to the site where he noted that one of his cows had been killed and six had been injured, three of which had to be sent immediately to slaughter. Several apple trees had also been damaged, but Loncke was not too concerned about that as the trees belonged to the Duke of Broglie. The Duke's estate manager, Francois Laudet, later determined that seventy-five mature cider apple trees had been destroyed, along with 130 metres of barbed wire. The damages would amount to 125,000 francs.

The police arrived on site at about 7.00 a.m. and took charge. Soon after the Broglie fire brigade arrived. By then four bodies had been pulled from the wreckage and the fire-fighters were able to recover three further bodies which were badly disfigured. The police informed Captain Giraud, the commanding officer of the French Air Force base at Orly, now the airport south of Paris. He immediately drove the ninety miles from Orly to make a preliminary investigation of the crash site. He established that the crashed aircraft was a British airliner and he informed the British Embassy in Paris. Meanwhile, the police attempted to identify the seven bodies which had been recovered using passports found in the wreckage. They were:

Captain Copeland

First Officer d'A. Sephton

Navigating Officer L.R. Hastings DFC

Radio Officer J. Mossop DFC DFM

Radio Officer Blades

Steward F.W. Roberts

Steward K.L. Bloxham

The name of Radio Officer Blades was actually added to the list the next day; his passport having been partially destroyed, delaying identification. Navigating Officer G.F. Wimbury had serious injuries, and he died three hours after Pierre Bouillier delivered him to the hospital at Bernay. Mr W.J. Smith, the passenger who had boarded the aircraft at Lydda, had only minor injuries; he was the only person to survive the crash. Jack Mossop's flight bag had been thrown out of the fuselage as it collapsed. As a result, his log book was recovered undamaged and it was sent on with his other effects to Hilda. Jack's pencilled notes and recommendations relating the R/O Blades were still tucked into the log book. The Paris correspondent of *The Times* of London was quick off the mark and filed a reasonably accurate report on the crash which appeared in the paper the next day. By then, Hilda had been informed of her husband's death. Bill Lloyd was called out of a lecture at Hurn to be informed.

The British Official nearest to the crash site was the His Majesty's Consul in Rouen, about fifty miles away. He went to the site, taking with him two RAF officers who were based near Rouen and also one officer and three other ranks from No. 35 Graves Registration Unit who volunteered to guard the wreck. Rouen had been in the midst of the fighting following the D-Day landing two years earlier, and the task of identifying and burying the dead was not yet over. The Consul stayed at the site until a BEA team led by Mr Baldock arrived from Paris. He then returned to Rouen where he wrote a report to the Air Attaché at the British Embassy in Paris. Meanwhile, Baldock arranged for the removal of the bodies to the mortuary at Bernay Hospital and began to make arrangements for funerals in France or alternatively transport of the bodies to the United Kingdom. As part of this process, Hilda was asked whether she wished to have Jack's body brought back to England. She asked whether it was recognisable, and was told that it was not. She then asked where the pilot was to be buried. Jack had once told her that he would wish to be buried with his crew if they had been shot down on active service. Captain Copeland, it turned out, was to be buried in the cemetery at Bernay and that is where Jack's grave can also be found, alongside those of the two pilots Copeland and Sephton and the navigator Wimbury and others in his last crew. They were buried on 23 August 1946. The members of both the British and French investigatory teams attended the funeral service which was conducted by a RAF chaplain, and the Reverend W. Dunbar, Chaplain to the British Embassy in Paris, who gave an address, which was as comforting as the circumstances allowed.

My friends,

At this point of the Service I want to say something which I hope may help to comfort those who mourn in England. As we stand here in the presence of this tragic sorrow, their hearts and thoughts are with us. I want them to know something of this tribute of sympathy and respect which has been paid by you all in an attempt to share their bitter grief. I want them to know of you good French people of Bernay and the way your Council has granted a free space in this cemetery for this sacred burial. I want them to know of the presence here of those who represent the British Consul at Rouen and the Military Attaché in Paris and the representatives of BOAC. But I want them to know something more. This Christian burial service is not simply an occasion to pay tributes of respect and sympathy; it is an occasion on which we confess one of the great articles of the Christian Faith. We believe in the Resurrection of the Dead and the Life Everlasting. We believe that when our Dear Ones are taken from us, they enter a realm where the dimensions of Time and Space do not exist. We believe that they are for ever with the Lord and that our Lord is for ever with us and therefore to those who mourn in England we want them to know that their Dear Ones are for ever with them, 'closer to them than breathing'. I hope that in some way a report of this Service may help them in this dark hour of their sorrow. And to our Brothers who have been taken away from us we say: 'may peace be with you, may light perpetual shine upon you and may you have joy for evermore.'

Four days later, the Reverend Dunbar wrote a letter of condolence to Hilda, stressing the great respect shown by the French people. They had lined the route and at the head of the cortège was a company of Old French Soldiers. The British Air Attaché had

161

sent a representative, BOAC had been represented by the Paris BEA station manager and both the British pro-consul and the military attaché at Rouen were also in attendance. A week or so later, the British Legion sent Hilda a photograph of Jack's grave stone. The inscription reads:

RADIO OFFICER

J MOSSOP DFC AND BAR DFM

BRITISH OVERSEAS AIRWAYS

CORPORATION

20TH AUGUST 1946 AGE 26

REMEMBERED ALWAYS

Meanwhile, an investigation had begun to find out what had caused the crash. Because they did not fly to destinations in Europe, BOAC were represented in France by the staff of BEA. The British Embassy therefore requested the BEA Station Manager at Le Bourget airport to conduct an initial enquiry, a task given to Mr Sol.

At 10.30 a.m. on 20 August the French Air Security Department had sent a telegram to BOAC in London informing them of the crash and stating that the Chief of the French Security Department was on his way to the crash site to begin an investigation. BOAC copied the telegram to the Chief Inspector of Accidents in the Ministry of Civil Aviation (MCA). Because the crash was on French soil, the French authorities would be responsible for the formal investigation under the rules of the newly established International Civil Air Organisation (ICAO). However, as the country of both manufacture and registration, the UK was involved as an interested party. The process was initiated in UK through a letter from BOAC to the Permanent Secretary of the Ministry of Civil Aviation (MCA). The letter was written and no doubt delivered by hand on 21 August, the day after the crash. It began 'In accordance with the Air Navigation (Investigation of Accidents) Regulations...I regret to have to inform you that the above aircraft has met with an accident...'.

The letter goes on to give the nationality and registration mark of the aircraft, G-AGMF, the name of its owner, the name of the pilot, where the accident occurred and details of casualties. The letter finally confirms that next of kin have been informed. Most of this information had already been disseminated to those who needed it through telegrams sent from the Air Attaché in Paris. The MCA was a new government department, set up to develop the UK's civil aviation industry. Overall responsibility for air matters lay with the Air Ministry who took the lead in the investigation which now began. The senior inspector was Mr D.L. Craig. In support he had two inspectors from the MCA, Wing Commander Warren and Wing Commander Clifton. The Assistant Air Attaché in Paris, Air Commodore H.E. Walker, was notified by a telegram sent at 8.30 p.m. on 20 August, only about twelve hours after the time of the crash, that a special flight was arranged leaving London airport at 2.00 p.m. the following day. The Air Commodore was asked to ensure that the three inspectors were met at Le Bourget airport. Wing Commander Warren was issued with a certificate authorising him to carry, in a sealed bag, classified documents below the level of secret. It is not clear why they might need to carry classified documents, but it might have been connected with an issue which arose later.

The inspectors arrived in Paris on the evening of 21 August. The next morning was spent in establishing contacts with the French authorities. An official committee of enquiry had not at that stage been appointed, but the arrival of the British team hastened events, and by 12.30 p.m. the next day, the Minister of Public Works had appointed a committee of two, Captain Giraud of the French Air Force, who had conducted the preliminary investigation the previous day, and M Bellonte. The joint investigation team obtained a report of Captain Giraud's findings, and then they travelled to the scene of the crash in the afternoon of 22 August.

On arrival at the crash site, the two MCA inspectors had access to Mr Baldock's work in establishing the basic attributes of the crash. From the evidence of the witnesses he had established that the aircraft had flown over the farm house at Beauvais at an altitude of about 100 feet. It hit level ground planted with mature apple trees about 700 yards from the farmhouse. Parts of the aircraft were found in an area 600 yards long and 200 yards wide. The charred bodies of Captain Copeland, Radio Officer Blades and Steward Roberts were found in what remained of the cockpit which was under the burnt remains of the port wing. Jack Mossop died in the fuselage, probably in the radio officer's position behind the cockpit. Mr Smith, the BOAC Operations officer travelling as a passenger was in hospital but doing well. Mr Smith was in fact a minor hero. Despite his own injuries, it was he who had pulled the navigation officer out of the wreckage, although he sadly died later.

During the next day, 23 August, Craig and his helpers examined the wrecked aircraft and marked the locations of large components on a plan of the site, breaking only to attend the funeral service in Bernay. On the third day of the investigation they visited the surrounding countryside and interviewed witnesses who had not previously given evidence to the local police or Captain Giraud's initial investigation. It was becoming clear that the weather had been a significant factor in the crash. Craig therefore returned to Paris, and the next day spent the morning at the French Meteorological Office. He examined the synoptic charts for the days previous to the crash so that he could understand the weather conditions at the time, with particular emphasis on the potential for turbulence, icing and lightning. He then arranged for more detailed meteorological data to be sent to London for further analysis.

Back at the site, the inspectors now had a copy of the report prepared by the BEA Paris Station Engineer, Mr Sol. This led them to request the radio message logs of the UK W/T Overseas Area Control at Gloucester and of the BOAC listening post. There was now no further need to inspect the wreckage. The BEA engineers were authorised to arrange for the removal and disposal of the debris. The BOAC logo on the tail was defaced and the wreckage was sold by weight, 10,150 kg at four francs per kilogram yielded 40,600 francs, about a third of the amount which BOAC would pay in compensation to the Duke of Broglio for the death of four cows, seventy-five apple trees and 130 metres of barbed wire.

Mr Craig returned to UK to write his report, which would be for internal information only, since the authoritative report would have to be issued by an agent of the French government. It is clear from the papers in the MCA file that the picture in Craig's mind was one of an aircraft crew unaware of the weather ahead of them. As we have already noted, the forecast given to the aircraft captain at Lydda was generally benign. Severe icing would be a hazard if he flew through the cumulonimbus cloud expected at altitudes up to 20,000 feet between Sardinia and the south coast of France, but the Lancastrian had an operational ceiling of 23,000 feet so he could easily climb over this front. Once over France, the weather was expected to be relatively benign. Copeland had mentioned to his one passenger, Mr Smith, that he would fly at 8,500 feet, presumably when not climbing over potential icing conditions. Of course, Copeland was not in command. He had been told to give the maximum amount of handling and freedom of decision making to First Officer Sephton. Copeland had taken a rest on a bunk in the cabin before they passed Malta, but it is not clear whether he was leaving all decisions to Sephton as they progressed beyond Malta. Jack (or perhaps R/O Blades) was asked to obtain a weather forecast from Malta to Istres. When received, this forecast mostly agreed with their original forecast from Lydda; if anything it suggested better conditions than they had expected. The forecast cold front was not particularly active. However, what they did not know was that there was another cold front behind it. This unexpected front was severe and characterised by severe turbulence in cumulonimbus clouds up to 6,500 feet, with severe icing above. Between the two fronts the weather was relatively benign, with no low cloud and broken clouds at medium level. The transition into the area of severe turbulence was sudden.

At 0431 Greenwich Mean Time (GMT), either Jack or R/O Blades asked for a weather forecast for landing at London Heathrow. Gloucester responded at 0448 GMT with:

Landing forecast for London Airport for 0600 GMT: QFE 1008, visibility 2 miles, cloud 5/10 at 1600 ft, 3/10 at 800 ft, surface wind NNW 10 miles/hour.

There was nothing in that reply to cause alarm, but six minutes later at 0454 GMT they asked for a landing forecast for Hurn airfield. Gloucester said they would send it, which they did at 0508 GMT. However there was no acknowledgment from the aircraft. Gloucester called again at 0510, and again at 0513, and again at 0518, and again at 0525, and then almost continuously until 0923 GMT.

It would have been impossible to deduce what was happening on G-AGMF if Mr Smith, the sole passenger had not survived the crash. He had been sleeping in the passenger compartment, but he woke up at 0455 GMT, thirteen minutes before Gloucester sent the second weather forecast. The flight had been smooth and everything had been in order, but the aircraft was now flying through thick black cloud. The only other person in the passenger cabin was Navigation Officer Winbury, who woke up at about 0510 GMT, just after Gloucester sent the forecast for a landing at Hurn. Winbury sat on the bunk below the one Mr Smith was using, exchanged a few words with him and went to the lavatory. He returned about fifteen minutes later and Smith then went to the lavatory. He filled the basin with water and began to wash. He then felt an unusual movement of the aircraft, as though the tail was rising rapidly. The time by his watch would then have been about 0529 GMT. Holding on to grab handles, he looked out of the window and saw the ground. A field looked like the size of a postage stamp, and he reckoned that they were at about 2,000 to 3,000 feet above the ground. The aircraft then dived, and Smith assumed that the pilot was trying to dive through a break in the cloud. The aircraft levelled out, and Mr Smith tried to continue his wash, but the aircraft lurched violently and he was thrown back. There was then a severe vibration at the rear of the aircraft, followed by another dive and then the engines went to full power. From the lavatory cubicle window, on the starboard side of the fuselage, Smith could see the ground and he estimated that the aircraft was banked 30° to starboard. At this point Mr Smith became unconscious. When he recovered, his watch was reading 0540 GMT. Evidence from the sole survivor and witnesses on the ground indicate that the aircraft hit the ground at 0530 GMT. The local time was 0630. Smith was unconscious for about ten minutes. When he regained consciousness, despite being in severe shock, he tried first to find a fire extinguisher to tackle the flames which were preventing access to a hole in the fuselage through which he could see Navigation Officer Winbury. Pierre Despinoy and Maurice Legas then arrived and the three of them managed to extricate Winbury. Mr Smith was then driven with the dying Winbury by Pierre Bouillier to the hospital at Bernay.

Apart from severe shock, Smith had only minor injuries and two days later he was able to provide reliable evidence to the investigating officers which corroborated their findings from examination of the crash site. The 30° bank to starboard which Smith had noted was consistent with the right wing hitting the lower part of the trunk of a tree whilst the corresponding trees in the row on the left side of the aircraft's progress were, at that point, untouched. There were some taller trees ahead in the aircraft's path, and it is possible that the pilot banked to starboard in an attempt to avoid them. The throttles were fully open and the engines' speed controls were at maximum. The trailing radio aerial was extended; its last use may have been to receive the transmission from Gloucester at 0508 GMT, which was not acknowledged by Jack – it can be assumed that Jack was in the wireless operator's cabin at this stage, given the emergency then developing. By the time he had written the message out and passed it to the captain, events would have become critical. The starboard wing hit the ground first and the whole aircraft disintegrated. The largest piece left intact was the tail, including the fuselage aft of the forward lavatory – Smith was lucky in going to the rear lavatory. Even so, the cubicle was upside down by the time he came round. Indeed, the whole tail of the aircraft was upside down and facing where it had come from. The inspectors found no evidence of malfunction in any of the aircraft's systems. So what went wrong?

Mr Craig's discussions with the French National Meteorological Office confirmed that, as forecast, a cold front had moved eastwards over northern France, but this was followed by a very pronounced secondary cold front, which was lying parallel to the intended flight path of G-AGMF between Marseille and Le Havre. Weather conditions ahead of this front had been very unstable over a very wide belt. There would be freezing air conditions between 5,000 and 6,500 feet, with a high likelihood of icing. Broken cloud could extend from 450 feet to

12,000 feet with 10/10 cumulonimbus cloud. It is not clear why the crew of G-AGMF did not know about this second front. They clearly felt its impact as they flew north, for it forced them to descend into high ground. Mr Craig concluded that there was no fire on board, there was no mechanical malfunction, radio communication was satisfactory, the aircraft was on track and there were no difficulties with navigation. However, the weather was bad, and the captain omitted to ask for an up-to-date weather forecast for the Marseille to UK leg of the flight.

Overall, Craig was unable to establish the cause of the crash through insufficient evidence. Instead, he offered four plausible explanations, in order of plausibility:

(i) The pilot wanted to 'break cloud' either to avoid the cumulonimbus or to establish his position accurately. He saw the ground through a hole in the cloud and made for the hole turning approximately 90° to port. The ground was actually the bottom of the Charentonne valley, where the township of Broglie is situated. Having dived through the hole in a westerly direction, he was faced with the high ground on the other side of the valley he was crossing and was forced to pull back so sharply as to cause the aircraft to stall. He checked the ensuing loss of height and control by opening up the engines, but insufficient ground clearance was available to effect a recovery.

(ii) The aircraft entered a cumulonimbus and got out of control.

(iii) The aircraft was forced down by icing.

(iv) The auto-pilot put the aircraft into a sudden or gradual dive and corrective measures were not applied in time.

The only one of these four explanations which is evidence-based is the first. The other three are entirely speculative, even though they may be plausible. It could also be considered speculative to consider who was in command and sitting in the first pilot's seat when the Lancastrian crashed. There was a vast difference between the levels of experience of the two pilots. Captain Copeland had 1,822 hours as a first pilot with Imperial Airways and BOAC, 415 of them at night, and nearly all in multi-engined aircraft. He also had a total of 2,240 hours as second pilot. First Officer Sephton had only 37 hours as first pilot and 135 as second pilot with BOAC, of which only 56 had been at night. Most of his flying experience had been with the RAF in single-seat Vultee aircraft used for dive-bombing, target towing and ancillary tasks. It will be recalled that Copeland had been given written instructions that Sephton should be given the maximum amount of handling (of the aircraft) and freedom of decision. Was it Sephton or Copeland who failed to obtain an up-dated weather forecast for the last leg home? And which one was in the first pilot's seat? Unlike the Lancaster, the Lancastrian had dual flight controls so even if Sephton was in the first pilot's seat it would have been possible for Copeland to take over. The sudden change in conditions created circumstances which required a sudden descent. When coned by searchlights over Essen on 3 April 1943 (Jack's Op. 46), Hoover followed Jack's advice to dive to escape the flak. But Hoover was a first class pilot in an aircraft designed for survival with a very experienced crew. The emergency came on very quickly in G-AGMF. The sudden change in weather conditions would challenge any pilot. Perhaps the crew were unlucky that the junior pilot happened to be at the controls just at the time when conditions so rapidly deteriorated. Or perhaps the two pilots and the two navigators on board could not agree on the best course of action.

The request for a weather forecast for Hurn could indicate concern that they may not have enough fuel to reach Heathrow. The most likely cause of such a concern would have been a realisation that headwinds had held them back, and the obvious solution was to divert to Hurn, about 100 miles nearer than Heathrow. The timeline of events supports such a theory:

0454	G-AGMF requests weather at Hurn
0455	Mr Smith wakes up
0510	Gloucester message with Hurn weather not acknowledged by G-AGMF
0529	First 'lurch' noted by Smith
0530	Aircraft hits the ground

We have to recognise that Mr Smith was using his own watch to judge the time of events and there could be discrepancy of several minutes between his record of time and that given by the chronometers in the cockpit and by messages from the Gloucester radio station. The sixteen minutes between the request for Hurn weather and the response from Gloucester, must surely have been a period of realisation in G-AGMF that they were in deep trouble. The next period, of less than twenty minutes if Mr Smith's watch was running ahead of GMT, sealed their fate. There was no need to acknowledge Gloucester's message; it had become irrelevant.

There is no consideration in the accident report of the flying limitation included in the *Lancastrian Pilots Notes* on the need to avoid excessive loads on the elevators when recovering from dives. This omission probably reflects circumstances which, given the cloud conditions, gave the aircraft insufficient time to recover regardless of elevator loading.

Craig's report was not, of course, the authoritative version of what happened. That would be given by the French inspectors and it would be some time before it was available. Meanwhile the investigation grew another dimension. Craig signed off his report on 25 April 1946. Three days later an official identified as D.G.T.S. (probably standing for Director-General of Technical Services) in the MCA received a loose minute from his minister:

The Prime Minister is interested in the B.O.A.C. Lancastrian crash. Have we any advance news of the cause? If so, let No. 10 know.

The Prime Minister at the time was Clement Atlee, who had deposed Winston Churchill in the first post-war General Election. In passing, it is interesting that the Prime Minister's staff in No. 10 Downing used the word 'crash' rather than accident, whilst other officials call it an accident. The PM's staff were, of course correct – the incident should not be called an accident until an investigation report determining that the crash was accidental was submitted and accepted.

A second minute on the same piece of paper, dated 29 August is directed at the Accident Investigation Branch in MCA:

1. From our telephone conversation this afternoon (Stewart-Tweedle) it is understood that you have reached no conclusion regarding the cause of the crash of the B.O.A.C. Lancastrian crash in France.

2. In order to save time it is therefore requested that as soon as information is to hand you will deal direct with the above loose minute from Lord Winster

A week later, on 5 September, the Director of Safety in MCA had to fend off another enquiry from the Prime Minister on the progress of the French investigation and on 25 September Air Commodore Vernon Brown, the Chief Inspector (Accidents) in the MCA wrote a loose minute to his own minister, slipping into premature statements about an accident:

I understand that the Prime Minister is interested in the above accident and has asked for advance information as to the cause.

The actual investigation of the accident was undertaken by the French in accordance with International agreement. A representative from this branch co-operated with them during the investigation. While the French have not yet sent us a copy of their report and its findings, it seems likely that the cause of the accident will be attributed to errors on the part of the pilot rather to any failure of the aircraft or its equipment.

The loose minute goes on to give the pertinent circumstances of the crash, based on the Craig report. Apparently, this did not satisfy the Prime Minister's staff. Clement Attlee spoke to Lord Winster, the Minister of Civil Aviation, who was obliged to write to Attlee on 27 September. His letter merely repeated the contents of Vernon Brown's minute of 15 September. Attlee did not leave it there. Three weeks later, Mr Poland, Attlee's private secretary, wrote another loose minute to the Chief Inspector of Accidents:

The Prime Minister is interested in the accident which occurred on a training flight to the B.O.A.C. Lancastrian in France a little time ago, and has asked whether the French have made any further progress in the investigation of this accident.

The response was:

1. In respect of this accident and any further to my R.20603/46/C.A.102 of September 25th. a letter was received yesterday from the French Accidents Inspector who is responsible for the drafting of this report. The letter was written from Oslo and he says that if nothing interferes with his plans, he hopes to be back in Paris by Wednesday, that is to say today. He adds that he hopes his report will be completed by the end of this weekend that he will keep us informed.

2. I imagine, therefore, that we shall not receive it for about a fortnight.

And what was the compulsion on the Prime Minister which required him to enquire into what was a relatively trivial incident, at least to those not directly affected by the crash of G-AGMF? The answer may well be found in a short piece published in *The London Evening Standard* on 29 November 1946:

B.O.A.C. Line to Palestine May Close

News that British Overseas Airways are likely to close their Palestine service within the next few days, owing to threats of Jewish terrorist sabotage, reached London last night.

Threats to sabotage planes at Lydda Airport were received from Irgun Zvai Leumi.

Pilots of this airline believe that sabotage wrecked the training Lancastrian 30 miles north of Paris about six weeks ago.

It is thought in Jerusalem that the British airline are considering leaving Palestine, but officials in London said last night: 'We know nothing of any threats or any suggestion to close Lydda.'

Only four months had past since the bombing of the King David Hotel in Jerusalem. It would have been a major embarrassment to the British Government if Irgun had been able to place a bomb on a BOAC aircraft.

We have already noted the security threat to British people which had prevented the crew of G-AGMF leaving the airport at Lydda. However, there was no evidence of an explosion on the aircraft as they flew to their deaths over France, nor of any malfunction which could have been the result of sabotage. The real extent of the threat would have been known to the Prime Minister through his briefings from MI6. His repeated demands for information on the progress of the crash investigation were very likely occasioned by concerns that the terrorists might have been able to place a bomb on board. The perceived threat did have one consequence: the file raised in the MCA remained classified SECRET for many years after the event.

In fact, the MCA did have advance information of what Bellonte had in mind as the most likely cause of the crash. His provisional conclusions were written down in a note translated into English on 29 August 1946, on a single foolscap sized page marked SECRET. His conclusions at this stage were almost identical to Craig's report:

> Faced with a secondary cold front and cumulonimbus, it would appear that the pilot tried to take advantage of gaps in the area of fractocumulus, in order to get below cloud. During this manoeuvre, Mr Smith saw the ground and it appears that the crew did also.

Bellonte put a little more weight than Craig had on the error in estimating distance travelled due to the unexpected head wind, but he emphasised that the condition of the engines, airframe and other equipment did not appear to be in question.

Correspondence between London and Paris began to be somewhat tense. Bellonte could not, of course, be told of the possible terrorist factor and he rather resented the pressure being put on an investigation which almost from the start seemed to be leading to crew error. Eventually, Air Commodore Vernon Brown intervened and went to see Bellonte in Paris. His subsequent letter, dated 2 December 1946, indicates that there had been some sort of rapprochement:

> I have today sent you a signal giving the information you want...If there is anything else you require, please ask, but I

hope that this will be enough for you to complete your report.

Please accept my best thanks for your kindness to me in Paris last week and particularly to Mme Bellonte for the wonderful lunch party. When you come here this week or next I would like to reciprocate, but you must not expect that we can compete with Paris in respect with food!

Some things don't change. The signalled information was to confirm that wind speed and ground speed were both quoted in knots, and to provide the exact map coordinates of London Heathrow.

The formal report was finally delivered on 11 January 1947 in the form of an advance copy delivered to the British Embassy in Paris. An English language version was available in London on 17 January. Most of the report consists of material already assembled for the Craig report. Laid out in the new Provisional ICAO format, in twelve pages and eight annexes, it first provides details of the aircraft, its fitted equipment and its crew. It then describes the circumstances of the accident, based mostly on the statements of witnesses. The evidence from Mr Smith, the only survivor, is praised for its 'extreme objectivity'. The report emphasises the point that Mr Smith's survival hinged on the fact that the passenger's lavatory is a long way back in the fuselage of a Lancastrian. By implication, those further forward had little chance. Wing Commanders Warren and Clifton were also praised for their help during the initial phase of the investigation. Emphasis was placed on meteorological issues and there is a detailed drawing in an annex of the conditions at the time of the crash. The report concludes that the pilot believed that they had passed over the Normandy hills, and that it was safe to take advantage of broken cloud to descend to lower altitude, possibly to ensure that they could ascertain their position as they flew over the coast at or near Le Havre, where they had planned a change of course. Unfortunately, they had not passed over the Normandy Hills, and they hit the ground before they were able to recover from their miscalculation.

It was now correct to call the crash an accident, and the Prime Minister did not have to deal with the implications of another terrorist attack in Palestine.

Epilogue

I have now nearly reached the end of my story. What happened next? The answer is very little, at least in comparison with the events which I have described.

Jack's posting from 35 Squadron as soon as he had completed ninety operations broke the bonds of the crew. He remained in touch only with Cliff Hill, the air gunner and Bill Lloyd, the flight engineer. Both were awarded well deserved DFMs. Cliff finished his service in the RAF in the rank of warrant officer. Bill Lloyd was commissioned, and when the war ended in 1945 he followed Jack into BOAC. Cliff had thought that Jack was immortal. In his experience, no one survived ninety operations. Bravery is one of the minor themes of this story, and we have seen some significant examples. Jack won a medal for his action over Cuxhaven in the cold winter of 1941/42, flying in a sparsely fitted Hampden bomber. His bravery then was an immediate reaction to dangerous circumstances, but it was a different order of bravery which enabled aircrew to expose themselves to risk on a regular basis, with odds of survival which with time could clock up to odds of 10 to1 against.

Perhaps if British governments in the 1930s had been more active in building a strong military capability, the need for such bravery would not have occurred. The theme of politics touches this story, but I started the story at a time when the mistakes had been recognised and there was strong political will to resist aggression. One of the factors which led to the Allied victory was high resolve at the political level. The strategic aim was simple: to defeat Germany and to restore the sovereign states of Europe.

This aim was largely maintained during the years of war, but success led to another period of uncertainty in the form of the Cold War. Arguably it was the memory of the Second World War which kept the Cold War cold. Back in 1939, however, the British Government had few options. If the threat posed by Germany and its allies was to be met and overcome, it was essential that Britain took the war to the enemy. For a long time RAF Bomber Command was the only force which could prosecute that strategy. The men who fought in the air came from many countries, and many other men and women provided essential support on the ground. The particular contribution of Canadian aircrew, who found a second home in the villages of North Yorkshire, gave this story another theme. Jack flew in fifty-eight operations with a Canadian pilot, including twenty-two with another three Canadians.

Technological advances were essential for victory. This theme is too big to be given its full merit in this story, but without amazingly fast developments in electronics, particular in radar devices, the bomber crews would have rarely hit their targets. Bombing tactics evolved with the technology which provided better aircraft, bigger bombs and new electronic devices. By 1944 the tactics of the Pathfinders were heavily driven by technology.

As I promised, there has been a love theme running through this story. It started before our main protagonists appeared. The Mossop and the Charlton families were both inwardly dependent on themselves. The parents of those who died and those who suffered the death of a brother or husband, knew about this love. The bonds in families were more often strengthened than broken by such tragedy. Six weeks before the crash of G-AGMF, Jack, Hilda and Bill Lloyd, had gone to Oswestry for Cliff's wedding, at which Jack was the best man. They stayed overnight and Bill worked out the railway timetable from Bournemouth. By then Bill was at Hurn, training for a civilian air engineer licence. No one could afford a car; indeed none of them could even drive a car. On the way back they stopped in Bath for a few hours. Sightseeing was rare pleasure, but the photographs taken at the wedding and later in front of Bath Abbey show the three of them in a relaxed mood, with the anxiety of war dispelled. Many years later Bill admitted to me that he had suggested changing trains in

Bath not with sightseeing in mind but because he had a girl friend in Bath (but he would not say whether he actually found the girl-friend).

Bill stayed with BOAC and had a full career in civil aviation, retiring in 1977. Cliff Hill also had a long career in aviation; he died peacefully in 2005. Their pilot, Squadron Leader Hoover lives in Vancouver after his second stint of service with the RCAF. About half of the crew who flew with Jack, Bill Lloyd, and Cliff Hill in Hoover's crew are still alive as I write. Jack Mossop was twenty-six years old when he died, somewhat short of immortality, but he had faced long odds on survival since he first qualified as a Wireless Operator/Air Gunner. It is the time axis of the risk equation which unexpectedly brings the reaper. I said at the beginning that risk would be one of the main themes that run through this story.

Jack and Hilda played the central part in the love theme. Yet they hardly knew each other. They first met during the summer of 1943 and any subsequent courting was well supervised. They had seen each other during a few weekends in the summer and autumn of 1943, when they were allowed to talk to each other, but no more. Then there was the day when Jack arrived in Newcastle and put an engagement ring on her finger to finalise their courting. But in February 1944 Jack was posted to 35 Squadron at RAF Gravely, doubling the distance between them. He had two periods of leave during his time at Graveley. During the first, they married and had a seven-day honeymoon. During the next they stayed with Hilda's parents for a week. And that was it, apart from a weekend in St Neots when Jack came back from bombing a military depot in Belgium: less than three weeks of married life before they went to Bournemouth, and overall a total of 238 days of marriage spread over three years. Yet it was love which bound them and Hilda can recall every day. She was also about to find that the consequences of events are not always death or injury. Other consequences can result from a hazardous event such as an aircraft crash, including financial loss.

Jack had become an employee of BOAC on the day he agreed to help out on the training sortie in G-AGMF, but he was airborne before management and secretarial staff had arrived in the BOAC office. Jack may have been a BOAC employee, but he had not been able to sign the paperwork which would make him a member of BOAC's pension fund. On the other hand, he had left the RAFVR the previous day. His widow was thus not entitled to a war pension. Hilda eventually received £2,000 from a life accident insurance policy which covered all BOAC employees, and unpaid salary and allowances amounting to £28 17s 1d, but no pension. The pay-off was equivalent to over £50,000 in 2005; enough to buy a house, but not much to live on. With no other option available, she returned with me, to live with her parents in Medomsley. She was twenty-three years old (but that's a secret). I was eighteen months old. The train journey from Bournemouth to Newcastle upon Tyne took ten hours. Then we took the bus home.

Some time later, Hilda received through the post four war medals awarded posthumously to Flight Lieutenant Mossop: the 1939-45 Star, the Air Crew Europe Star with clasp 'France and Germany', the Defence Medal and the War Medal 1939-45. For reasons never satisfactorily explained, those who fought in Bomber Command during the Second World War were not awarded a campaign medal of their own.

Later still, Hilda married another Jack, whose surname was Robinson, changing both her name and mine in the process, and she gave birth to two more boys, my brothers Alan and Charles. She now lives in Northumberland.

Notes

Chapter 2
1. Sir John Slessor, *The Great Deterrent*, published by Cassell, 1956.
2. Technical details of RAF aircraft given in this account are taken from Owen Thetford, *Aircraft of the Royal Air Force since 1918*, 7th Revised Edition, published by Putnam.
3. As described in *So Many* published by W.H. Smith in 1995.

Chapter 3
1. I am indebted to my cousin Mary Fawcett, grand-daughter of Grace Mossop for some of these family details.

Chapter 4
1. John Terraine, *The Right of the Line*, Wordsworth Editions Ltd.
2. Sir Maurice Dean, quoted in Terraine, op. cit.
3. Sir Arthur Harris, *Bomber Offensive*, 1947 original version published by Greenhill Books.
4. Terraine, op. cit.

Chapter 5
1. Harris, op. cit.

Chapter 6
1. Terraine, op. cit.
2. Details of RAF Stations and Squadrons are, in part, taken from the RAF website.
3. Owen Thetford, op. cit.

4. Harris, op. cit.
5. Richard Morris, *Guy Gibson*, Viking Penguin Books Ltd., 1994.
6. Guy Gibson, *Enemy Coast Ahead – Uncensored* © RAF Museum Hendon, published by Crécy Publishing Ltd.
7. In some accounts of bomber operations confusion can arise because some aircraft took off after midnight on the day in which an operation had been planned. In this account, the date given for an operation is the day on which it was detailed and planned.
8. Statistics taken from Terraine, op. cit.
9. Terraine, op. cit.
10. Details of these awards are taken from *The Distinguished Flying Medal Register for the Second World War* compiled by Ian Tavender, published by Savannah Publications, 2000.
11. Details of the citation are taken from *Distinguished Flying Cross and How it was Won* by N. Carter, Savannah Publications, 1998.
12. From a table created for the *Air Member Training* on 16 November 1942, reproduced by Terraine, op. cit.

Chapter 7
1. Terraine, op. cit.
2. ibid.
3. Harris, op. cit.
4. John Sweetman, *Bomber Crew*, Little, Brown, 2004.

Chapter 8
1. Max Hastings, *Bomber Command*, Michael Joseph Ltd., 1979.
2. ibid.
3. *The National Trust Handbook for Members and Visitors*, 2006.
4. Michael P Wadsworth, *They Led the Way*, Highgate Publications (Beverley) Ltd.
5. Extracts from 106 Squadron's ORB and Gibson's flying log book are as given in Morris, op. cit.
6. Morris, op. cit. provides probably the best description of the Dambuster raid.
7. Some details from Sweetman, op. cit.
8. Hastings, op. cit.

9. ibid.
10. ibid.
11. Harris, op. cit.
12. ibid.
13. Hastings, op. cit.
14. *So Many* W.H. Smith, 1995.
15. Hastings, op. cit.
16. Rosemary Enright, *The Story of Nun Monkton*, D.P. Aykroyd, 1989.
17. Terraine, op. cit.

Chapter 9
1. Details from Newsletter No. 47 of the RAF Air Defence Museum, May 2006, article by the late Rex Boys.
2. Professor R.V. Jones, *Most Secret War*, Hamish Hamilton Ltd., 1978.
3. Details from Rowland White, *Vulcan 607*, Bantam Press, 2006.
4. Merril I. Skolnik, *Introduction to Radar Systems*, McGraw-Hill, 1962.
5. Jones, op. cit.
6. As described in *So Many*.
7. Details about Mahaddie are taken from *So Many*.

Chapter 10
1. Thetford, op. cit.
2. Wadsworth, op. cit.
3. Details from Air Publication 2062A, *Pilots and Flight Engineer's Notes Lancaster Marks I, III, and X*, promulgated by Order of the Air Council, Crown Copyright and reproduced by Crécy Publishing Ltd., by permission of Her Majesty's Stationery Office.
4. As described in *So Many*.
5. Jones, op. cit.
6. T.I. = Target Indicator, basically flares of differing colours either dropped immediately to the ground or hung from parachutes.
7. Jones, op. cit.
8. ibid.

9. Stephen Darlow, *D-Day Bombers: The Veterans' Story*, Grub Street.
10. ibid.
11. ibid.
12. AVM Cooke writing in *So Many*.
13. Terraine, op. cit.
14. I am indebted to Major M. Joost of the Directorate of History and Heritage of National Defence Headquarters, Ottawa, Ontario, for providing details of Squadron Leader Hoover's career.

Chapter 11
1. Hans Dollinger *The Decline and Fall of Nazi Germany and Imperial Japan*, translated from the German by Arnold Pomerans, Bonanza Books.
2. ibid.
3. Terraine, op. cit.

Chapter 12
1. Details from BAA website.
2. Kings Cross railway station.

Chapter 13
1. Richard A. Franks, *The Avro Lancaster – a comprehensive guide for the modeller*, SAM Publications, 2000.
2. AP 4154 A&B – P.N.
3. Details from Wikipedia website June 2006.

Appendix 1

Ranks in the Royal Air Force

Although the ranks in the Royal Air Force have not changed since 1945, their abbreviations have. This is a list of those currently in use.

Rank	Abbreviation
Commissioned ranks	
Marshal of the Royal Air Force	MRAF
Air Chief Marshal	ACM
Air Marshal	AM
Air Vice-Marshal	AVM
Air Commodore	A Cdre
Group Captain	Gp Capt
Wing Commander	Wg Cdr
Squadron Leader	Sqn Ldr
Flight Lieutenant	Flt Lt
Flying Officer	Fg Off
Pilot Officer	Plt Off
Non commissioned ranks	
Warrant Officer	WO
Flight Sergeant	FS
Chief Technician	Ch Tech
Sergeant	Sgt
Corporal	Cpl
Junior Technician	JT
Senior Aircraftman	SAC

Leading Aircraftman	LAC
Aircraftman 1	AC1
Aircraftman 2	AC2

Note: The term aircraftman now includes aircraftwoman.

Appendix 2

Jack Mossop's Ninety Operations in Chronological Order

49 Squadron		Scampton	Hampden			
Op	Date	Pilot	Duty	Tail No	Target	Comments
1	30/6/41	Sgt Huggett	AG	AD896	Dusseldorf	
2	3/7/41	Sgt Latty	AG	X3151	Bremen	
3	5/7/41	Sgt Latty	AG	X3185	Returned after 40 mins Starboard engine u/s	
4	8/7/41	Sgt Bunn	AG	AD980	Hamm	
5	10/7/41	Sgt Bunn	AG	AD980	Cologne	
6	12/7/41	Sgt Bunn	W/OP AG	AD980	Bremen	Landed at Mildenhall
7	14/7/41	Plt Off Harvey	AG	AD980	Heligoland	Gardening
8	16/7/41	Sgt Bunn	AG	AD980	Hamburg	
9	20/7/41	Sgt Bunn	AG	AD980	Aachen	Alternative target
10	23/7/41	Sgt Bunn	AG	AD980	Frankfurt	Diverted to Coningsby
11	25/7/41	Sgt Bunn	AG	AD980	Hanover	
12	28/7/41	Sgt Bunn	AG	AD980	Kiel bay	Gardening
13	2/8/41	Sgt Bunn	AG	AD980	Unable to locate target	Gardening
14	5/8/1	Sgt Bunn	AG	AD980	Karlsruhe	Fires observed
15	29/8/41	Plt Off Cooke	W/Op	AD805	Frankfurt	
16	31/8/41	Plt Off Cooke	W/OP	AD805	Cologne	Unable to find target–bombed searchlights
17	12/9//41	Plt Off Cooke	W/OP	AD980	Frankfurt	
18	15/9/41	Plt Off Cooke	W/OP	AD90	Willhelmshaven	
19	28/9/41	Plt Off Cooke	W/OP	AD979	Frankfurt	Landed at Dishforth
20	14/10/41	Sgt Latty	W/OP	AD979	Cologne	Landed at Martlesham Heath
21	20/10/41	Sgt Watt	W/OP	AD980	Frisians	Gardening – successful

22	3/11/41	Sgt Robinson	W/OP	HE372	Convoys off Frisians	
23	23/11/41	Plt Off Robinson	W/OP	AD980	Lorient (France nr Brest)	
24	26/11/41	Plt Off Robinson	W/OP	AD980	Emden	
25	30/11/41	Plt Off Robinson	W/OP	AD979	Hamburg	Land mine
26	8/12/41	Plt Off Robinson	W/OP	AE396	Aachen	
27	12/12/41	Plt Off Robinson	W/OP	AD979	Cuxhaven	Crashed at Bircham Newton
28	28/12/41	Plt Off Robinson	W/OP	AE396	Huls	Rubber factory; land mine
29	5/1/42	Plt Off Robinson	W/OP	AE396	Brest	
30	10/1/42	Plt Off Robinson	W/OP	AE396	Brest	

16 OTU   Upper Heyford   Hampden

Op	Date	Pilot	Duty	Tail No	Target	Comments
31	30/5/42	FS Riley	W/OP	P2138	Cologne	Op Millenium
32	1/6/42	FS Riley	W/OP	P2138	Essen	Turned back – starboard engine u/s

76 Squadron   Linton-on-Ouse   Halifax

Op	Date	Pilot	Duty	Tail No	Target	Comments
33	16/2/43	Sgt Hoover	W/OP	BB282	Lorient	
34	18/2/43	Sgt Hoover	W/OP	BB282	Frisians	Gardening
35	19/2/43	Sgt Hoover	W/OP	W7820	Wilhelmshaven	
36	25/2/43	Sgt Hoover	W/OP	BB238	Nuremburg	
37	26/2/43	Sgt Hoover	W/OP	BB238	Cologne	
38	28/2/43	Sgt Hoover	W/OP	BB238	St Nazaire	
39	1/3/43	Sgt Hoover	W/Op	BB238	Berlin	
40	3/3/43	Sgt Hoover	W/Op	BB238	Hamburg	
41	5/3/43	Sgt Hoover	W/Op	BB238	Essen	
42	8/3/43	Sgt Hoover	W/Op	BB238	Nuremburg	
43	9/3/43	Sgt Hoover	W/Op	BB238	Munich	
44	12/3/43	Sgt Hoover	W/Op	BB238	Essen	
45	26/3/43	Sgt Hoover	W/Op	BB238	Duisberg	
46	3/4/43	Sgt Hoover	W/Op	BB238	Essen	
47	4/4/43	Sgt Hoover	W/Op	DT541	Kiel	
48	14/4/43	Sgt Hoover	W/Op	BB365	Stuttgart	
49	16/4/43	Sgt Hoover	W/Op	BB365	Pilsen	Skoda works
50	20/4/43	Sgt Hoover	W/Op	BB365	Stettin	
51	26/4/43	Sgt Hoover	W/Op	DK173	Duisberg	
52	28/4/43	Sgt Hoover	W/Op	DK173	Kategat	Gardening
53	30/4/43	Sgt Hoover	W/Op	DK137	Essen	
54	4/5/43	Sgt Hoover	W/Op	DK137	Dortmund	

35 Squadron   Graveley   Lancaster Mk III

Op	Date	Pilot	Duty	Tail No	Target	Comments
55	22/3/44	Fg Off Hoover	W/OP	Q	Frankfurt	
56	24/3/44	Fg Off Hoover	W/OP	Q	Berlin	Landed at Wyton
57	26/3/44	Fg Off Hoover	W/OP	O	Essen	Good raid
58	11/4/44	Fg Off Hoover	W/OP	O	Aachen	40 mins wait to land
59	27/4/44	Fg Off Hoover	W/OP	O	Freidrichsafen	Back from leave
60	30/4/44	Fg Off Hoover	W/OP	R	Acheres	Pongo. One bomb hung up
61	3/5/44	Fg Off Hoover	Bomb-aimer	C	Mont Didier aerodrome	Pongo. combat with Ju88
62	6/5/44	Fg Off Hoover	Bomb-aimer	J	Mantes Gassicourt	Pongo. Marshalling yards
63	10/5/44	Fg Off Hoover	Bomb-aimer	C	Lens	Pongo. Marshalling yards
64	11/5/44	Fg Off Hoover	Bomb-aimer	C	Louvain	Pongo. Marshalling yards
65	19/5/44	Fg Off Hoover	Bomb-aimer	C	Boulogne	Marshalling yards
66	21/5/44	Fg Off Hoover	Bomb-aimer	C	Duisberg	Cloud over target; bombed Krefeld
67	22/5/44	Fg Off Hoover	Bomb-aimer	C	Dortmund	
68	24/5/44	Fg Off Hoover	Bomb-aimer	C	Aachen	
69	27/5/44	Fg Off Hoover	Bomb-aimer	C	Bourg-Leopold	Military camp
70	31/5/44	Fg Off Hoover	Bomb-aimer	C	Mont Couple	Radar jammer
71	2/6/44	Fg Off Hoover	Bomb-aimer	C	Trappes	Marshalling yard
72	5/6/44	Fg Off Hoover	Bomb-aimer	C	Maisy	Bombing coastal batteries. D-Day
73	6/6/44	Fg Off Hoover	Bomb-aimer	C	St Lo	DMB
74	8/6/44	Fg Off Hoover	Bomb-aimer	C	Mayenne	DMB
75	24/6/44	Flt Lt Hoover	Bomb-aimer	C	Rimeux	P-Plane site
76	27/6/44	Flt Lt Hoover	Bomb-aimer	C	Biennais	P-Plane site
77	30/6/44	Flt Lt Hoover	Bomb-aimer	C	Oisemont	DMB; P-Plane site
78	4/7/44	Flt Lt Hoover	Bomb-aimer	C	Villeneuve-St-George	Marshalling yard
79	6/7/44	Flt Lt Hoover	Bomb-aimer	C	Marquises	MB. Daylight. P-Plane site

80	7/7/44	Flt Lt Hoover	Bomb-aimer C	Army support near Caen	Daylight. Telegram from Montgomery
81	9/7/44	Flt Lt Hoover	Bomb-aimer C	Les Catelliers	MB. Daylight P-Plane site
82	11/7/44	Flt Lt Hoover	Bomb-aimer J	Gapennes	Daylight formation attack. P-Plane site
83	12/4/44	Flt Lt Hoover	Bomb-aimer M	Tours	DMB. Marshalling yard
84	18/7/44	Wg Cdr Daniels	Bomb-aimer C	Manneville	Daylight. Close Army support
85	23/7/44	Flt Lt Hoover	Bomb-aimer B	Kiel	
86	25/7/44	Flt Lt Hoover	Bomb-aimer C	Stuttgart	DMB, took over when MB did not turn up
87	28/7/44	Flt Lt Hoover	Bomb-aimer C	Stuttgart	
88	4/8/44	Flt Lt Hoover	Bomb-aimer C	Bec D'Ambes	MB. Daylight. Oil depot
89	6/8/44	Flt Lt Hoover	Bomb-aimer P	Foret de Nieppe	MB. Daylight. P-Plane site
90	8/8/44	Flt Lt Hoover	Bomb-aimer C	Aire-sur-Lys	MB. Fuel depot

Appendix 3

The Alice Hawthorn Anthem

There's a grand little pub
Only twelve miles from York
Where fellows can stretch out at ease
And relax from the turmoil of being at war
And do as they damn well please.

It's a snug little pub a haven of rest
With good humour the whole evening through
Where there's laughter and fun
When the day's work is done
And never a chance to feel blue.

There's always a welcome, a warm one at that
And beer that comes from the wood
A game of darts – bar billiards too
And corn on the cob if you are good.

You hang up your hat and order your meal,
And stretch out your legs to the blaze
And think to yourself how good it would be
To stay to end of your days.

To hundreds of lads who've come over the seas
To fly our big four-engined kites
The "Alice" means friendship and comfort and home
On non-operational nights.

The food is superb, it's wonderful how
Mrs Dodman cooks for a lot
It's a sight for sore eyes when the plates come in
At this perfectly heavenly spot!

189

To knock back a jar with Ted in the bar
It's just like heaven on earth
While Norman and Silver gossip all night
About farming for what it is worth.

The lads who come here again and again
They've no inclination to roam
They know very well that the Alice is swell
They look upon it as home.

So thanks Mr Ted and thanks Mrs Ted
And thank to the Joans big and small
We're grateful for all the kindness you've shown
We shall long remember it all.

Index.